THE PASSION TRANSLATION

THE PASSIONATE LIFE BIBLE STUDY SERIES

12-LESSON STUDY GUIDE

THE BOOKS OF

# 1&2 THESSALONIANS

FAITHFUL TO FINISH WELL

BroadStreet
PUBLISHING

BroadStreet Publishing® Group, LLC
Savage, Minnesota, USA
BroadStreetPublishing.com

TPT: The Books of 1 & 2 Thessalonians: 12-Lesson Bible Study Guide
Copyright © 2025 BroadStreet Publishing Group

9781424569700 (softcover)
9781424569717 (ebook)

All rights reserved. No part of this book may be reproduced in any form, except for brief quotations in printed reviews, without permission in writing from the publisher.

Unless indicated otherwise, all Scripture quotations are from The Passion Translation®. Copyright © 2017, 2018, 2020 by Passion & Fire Ministries, Inc. Used by permission. All rights reserved. ThePassionTranslation.com. Scripture quotations marked NIV are taken from The Holy Bible, New International Version® NIV® Copyright © 1973, 1978, 1984, 2011 by Biblica, Inc.™ Used by permission. All rights reserved worldwide.

General editor: Brian Simmons
Managing editor: William D. Watkins
Writer: Matthew A. Boardwell

Cover and interior by Garborg Design Works | garborgdesign.com

Printed in the United States of America

25 26 27 28 29 5 4 3 2 1

# Contents

# From God's Heart to Yours

"God is love," says the apostle John, and "Everyone who loves is fathered by God and experiences an intimate knowledge of him" (1 John 4:7). The life of a Christ-follower is, at its core, a life of love—God's love of us, our love of him, and our love of others and ourselves because of God's love for us.

And this divine love is reliable, trustworthy, unconditional, other-centered, majestic, forgiving, redemptive, patient, kind, and more precious than anything else we can ever receive or give. It characterizes each person of the Trinity—Father, Son, and Holy Spirit—and so is as limitless as they are. They love one another with this eternal love, and they reach beyond themselves to us, created in their image with this love.

How do we know such incredible truths? Through the primary source of all else we know about the one God—his Word, the Bible. Of course, God reveals who he is through other sources as well, such as the natural world, miracles, our inner life, our relationships (especially with him), those who minister on his behalf, and those who proclaim him to us and others. But the fullest and most comprehensive revelation we have of God and from him is what he has given us in the thirty-nine books of the Hebrew Scriptures (the Old Testament) and the twenty-seven books of the Christian Scriptures (the New Testament). Together, these sixty-six books present a compelling and telling portrait of God and his dealings with us.

It is these Scriptures that *The Passionate Life Bible Study Series* is all about. Through these study guides, we—the editors and writers of this series—seek to provide you with a unique and welcoming opportunity to delve more deeply into God's precious Word, encountering there his loving heart for you and all the others he loves. God wants you to know him more deeply, to love him more devoutly, and to share his heart with others more frequently and freely. To accomplish this, we have based this study guide series on The Passion Translation of the Bible, which strives to "reintroduce the passion and fire of the Bible to the English reader. It doesn't merely convey the literal meaning of words. It expresses God's passion for people and his world by translating the original, life-changing message of God's Word for modern readers." It has been created to "kindle in you a burning desire to know the heart of God, while impacting the church for years to come."[1]

In each study guide, you will find an introduction to the Bible book it covers. There you will gain information about that Bible book's authorship, date of composition, first recipients, setting, purpose, central message, and key themes. Each lesson following the introduction will take a portion of that Bible book and walk you through it so you will learn its content better while experiencing and applying God's heart for your own life and encountering ways you can share his heart with others. Along the way, you will come across a number of features we have created that provide opportunities for more life application and growth in biblical understanding.

## Experience God's Heart

This feature focuses questions on personal application. It will help you live out God's Word and to bring the Bible into your world in fresh, exciting, and relevant ways.

## Share God's Heart

This feature will help you grow in your ability to share with other people what you learn and apply in a given lesson. It provides guidance on using the lesson to grow closer to others and to enrich your fellowship with others. It also points the way to enabling you to better listen to the stories of others so you can bridge the biblical story with their stories.

## The Backstory

This feature provides ancient historical and cultural background that illuminates Bible passages and teachings. It deals with then-pertinent religious groups, communities, leaders, disputes, business trades, travel routes, customs, nations, political factions, ancient measurements and currency…in short, anything historical or cultural that will help you better understand what Scripture says and means.

## Word Wealth

This feature provides definitions for and other illuminating information about key terms, names, and concepts, and how different ancient languages have influenced the biblical text. It also provides insight into the different literary forms in the Bible, such as prophecy, poetry, narrative history, parables, and letters, and how knowing the form of a text can help you better interpret and apply it. Finally, this feature highlights the most significant passages in a Bible book. You may be encouraged to memorize these verses or keep them before you in some way so you can actively hide God's Word in your heart.

## Digging Deeper

This feature explains the theological significance of a text or the controversial issues that arise and mentions resources you can use to help you arrive at your own conclusions. Another way to dig deeper into the Word is by looking into the life of a biblical character or another person from church history, showing how that man or woman incarnated a biblical truth or passage. For instance, Jonathan Edwards was well known for his missions work among native American Indians and for his intellectual prowess in articulating the Christian faith, Florence Nightingale for the reforms she brought about in healthcare, Irenaeus for his fight against heresy, Billy Graham for his work in evangelism, Moses for the strength God gave him to lead the Hebrews and receive and communicate the law, and Deborah for her work as a judge in Israel. This feature introduces to you figures from the past who model what it looks like to experience God's heart and share his heart with others.

## The Extra Mile

While The Passion Translation's notes are extensive, sometimes students of Scripture like to explore more on their own. In this feature, we provide you with opportunities to glean more information from a Bible dictionary, a Bible encyclopedia, a reliable Bible online tool, another ancient text, and the like. Here you will learn how you can go the extra mile on a Bible lesson. And not just in study either. Reflection, prayer, discussion, and applying a passage in new ways provide even more opportunities to go the extra mile. Here you will find questions to answer and applications to make that will require more time and energy from you—if and when you have them to give.

As you can see above, each of these features has a corresponding icon so you can quickly and easily identify them.

You will find other helps and guidance through the lessons of these study guides, including thoughtful questions, application suggestions, and spaces for you to record your own reflections, answers, and action steps. Of course, you can also write in your own journal, notebook, computer document, or other resource, but we have provided you with space for your convenience.

Also, each lesson will direct you toward the introductory material and numerous notes provided in The Passion Translation. There each Bible book contains a number of aids supplied to help you better grasp God's words and his incredible love, power, knowledge, plans, and so much more. We want you to get the most out of your Bible study, especially using it to draw you closer to the One who loves you most.

Finally, at the end of each lesson you'll find a section called "Talking It Out." This contains questions and exercises for application that you can share, answer, and apply with your spouse, a friend, a coworker, a Bible study group, or any other individuals or groups who would like to walk with you through this material. As Christians, we gather together to serve, study, worship, sing, evangelize, and a host of other activities. We grow together, not just on our own. This section will give you ample opportunities to engage others with some of the content of each lesson so you can work it out in community.

We offer all of this to support you in becoming an even more faithful and loving disciple of Jesus Christ. A disciple in the ancient world was a student of her teacher, a follower of his master. Students study, and followers follow. Jesus' disciples are to sit at his feet and listen and learn and then do what he tells them and shows them to do. We have created *The Passionate Life Bible Study Series* to help you do what a disciple of Jesus is called to do.

So go.

Read God's words.

Hear what he has to say in them and through them.

Meditate on them.

Hide them in your heart.

Display their truths in your life.

Share their truths with others.

Let them ignite Jesus' passion and light in all you say and do.

Use them to help you fulfill what Jesus called his disciples to do: "Now wherever you go, make disciples of all nations, baptizing them in the name of the Father, the Son, and the Holy Spirit. And teach them to faithfully follow all that I have commanded you. And never forget that I am with you every day, even to the completion of this age" (Matthew 28:19–20).

And through all of this, let Jesus' love nourish your heart and allow that love to overflow into your relationships with others (John 15:9–13). For it was for love that Jesus came, served, died, rose from the dead, and ascended into heaven. This love he gives us. And this love he wants us to pass along to others.

# What I Love about Paul's Letters to the Thessalonians

Paul's letters contain so much hope and grace, especially when you turn to 1 and 2 Thessalonians. They are full of encouragement and exhortation that will leave you richer in your spiritual life.

The apostle Paul brought the gospel to the important city of Thessalonica, with an estimated population of one hundred thousand. Originally named Thermai ("hot springs"), the city was renamed Thessalonica after Alexander the Great's half-sister. The city was home to a Jewish community as well as many cults and false religions.

During his second apostolic journey, after leaving Philippi, Paul and his team arrived at the wealthy city of Thessalonica, the capital of Macedonia. As he preached and taught in the synagogue, many Jews and God-fearing gentiles became believers and formed a congregation of Christ-followers (Acts 17:4).

Shortly after leaving the city, Paul sent Timothy back to ensure the believers were doing well and living faithfully by the truths of the gospel. When Timothy returned, he informed Paul of the great faith, hope, and love still burning in these believers' hearts. So Paul wrote them this letter, about two years after the church had been established, to comfort and strengthen their hearts.

So why do I love these letters? Let me start with 1 Thessalonians.

- This letter is one of the earliest known writings of the apostle Paul, which makes it perhaps the oldest Christian writing we have. It dates back to AD 50–51, only twenty years after Jesus was crucified and raised from the dead.

- There is great comfort and hope in 1 Thessalonians. The believers had let Paul know that they had questions about the second appearing of Christ, so Paul addressed that subject in his letter. This young church needed to hear from their spiritual father, Paul.

- In this deeply personal letter, Paul offers wise and practical advice on how to live our lives with gratitude, grace, and glory. He addresses the recipients as their "father" (2:11) and their "mother" (v. 7). Eight times he addresses the Thessalonian believers as his beloved "brothers and sisters." He even describes them as his "exhilarating joy" (v. 19). Such a treasure is found in the few pages of this letter.

And why do I love 2 Thessalonians? The Jesus followers in Thessalonica looked to Paul as their apostolic father and asked him to clarify the events surrounding "the day of the Lord." So Paul wrote to inspire idle people to engage themselves in making a living and presenting the gospel of Christ through the holy example of their changed lives.

- We all want to know what living in the last days before Jesus' second coming will be like. Paul's second letter to the Thessalonians gives us some answers. With only forty-seven verses, this book is packed with prophetic insight to strengthen and prepare us for those coming days. Not only does 2 Thessalonians give us information about what is ahead, but it is also a map to guide us through anything that might assail us as we approach the grand finale of all time—the appearing of our Lord Jesus Christ with his glorious messengers of fire!

- Although we spend our lives watching and waiting for his appearance, we must live every day for his glory.

We are to be alert, awake, and filled with his holiness as we draw closer to the fulfillment of the ages.

- This letter encourages us to stand our ground, be faithful to the end, and always make the message of Christ beautiful in our lives. We must do more than combat evil; we must live for Christ and expect his coming. He should find us living as passionate lovers of God, abandoned to him with all our heart.

We all need the truth of 2 Thessalonians today to keep our lives focused on what is truth as we look to Christ alone to be our strength, no matter how difficult the future may appear. One day we will each be able to personally thank the apostle Paul for writing this inspired letter.

May you be blessed as you study 1 and 2 Thessalonians!

*Brian Simmons*

LESSON 1

# Uprooted by a Riot

(Acts 16:6–17:14)

At first, the shouts and tumult went unheeded as little more than street noise while the little band of converts carried on their lively discussion about Jesus the Christ. Before long, however, the crescendo of angry voices outside climaxed abruptly with fierce pounding on the door of Jason's house. "Where is Paul of Tarsus? We demand to see him! We know he is staying here. Bring him out!"

This infant Christian church had a notion that this day was coming. From the day they first heard the apostle Paul and his friends preach the good news of Jesus in their city, they were promised that following Jesus would bring hardship. Now, hardship had come to their door, attempting to uproot the church in Thessalonica.

The apostles were not in, so their host, Jason, bravely went out to meet the mob. Scripture does not tell us where Paul was that day, but he did not intend to be in Thessalonica at all. His plan for this journey had been to minister in Asia Minor (modern Turkey) where he had previously initiated gospel missions among the churches of Galatia. But God intervened, redirecting him to Europe. This change of direction brought him to one of the most important seaports in Greece.

- *How did Paul decide to turn his mission toward Europe instead of continuing to evangelize in Asia (modern-day Turkey) (Acts 16:6–10)?*

- *In what important Macedonian city did Paul and Silas evangelize before coming to Thessalonica (vv. 11–12)?*

- *What kind of initial response did they receive (vv. 13–15)?*

As an observant Jew with a thorough knowledge of the Hebrew (Old Testament) Scriptures, Paul was prepared to instruct fellow Jews about Jesus, their awaited Messiah. As Jews had fanned out across the world, they established synagogues wherever there were ten Jewish men. Synagogues were easy to find in the Middle East, North Africa, and Asia Minor, but when the apostles turned their attention to Europe, these Jewish communities became sparser.[2]

That is why Paul went to a riverside prayer meeting in Philippi. Had there been a synagogue to preach in, he would have done so. Instead, he was content to join a prayer group just outside the city and tell the good news to the women gathered there. Perhaps only one family believed the message.

The reception in Philippi did not remain this warm, however. Before long, Paul performed the exorcism of a fortune-telling slave girl. Upon deliverance from her demonic spirit, she also lost her supernatural abilities, which infuriated her owners, who had been making money off her. They then took Paul and Silas for judgment before the local rulers. Without a trial, these two men were publicly flogged and summarily dumped in jail overnight (vv. 16–24).

Rather than moaning over the pain and indignity they had endured, Paul and Silas worshiped God that night while their fellow prisoners listened. Suddenly, a miraculous earthquake shook the jail, swung open the doors, and loosed all the prisoners' chains. The jailer assumed a jailbreak, and rather than facing certain severe punishment from the city council, he steeled himself to drive a dagger into his own chest. Paul surprised him with the welcome news that no one had escaped. This unexpected relief brought the jailer to his knees and into the Christian faith. By morning, his whole family professed faith in Christ (vv. 25–34).

- *After these events, what decision did the magistrates make about the apostles (vv. 35–36)?*

- *Did Paul welcome or resist this decision (v. 37)? Why? What did he demand?*

- *How did the magistrates react to the report of the officers? What did the magistrates ask Paul and Silas to do? How did the two missionaries comply (vv. 38–40)?*

- *How would you describe the reception and effectiveness of Paul and Silas in Europe to this point?*

## To Thessalonica

Leaving Philippi, Paul and Silas continued down the Roman highway called the Egnatian Way. This route was built under the orders of Macedonian proconsul Gnaeus Egnatius in the second century before Christ. The road linked Byzantium (now Istanbul) to the Adriatic coast. From there, a 150 km boat trip could deliver a traveler to the terminus of the Appian Way leading to Rome. From Philippi, Thessalonica was the next major city on this important road (17:1).

In Paul's day, Thessalonica was already a thriving city and the seat of government for the Roman province of Macedonia. Because of its navigable commercial seaport, Thessalonica has been a principal center for trade for more than two thousand years.

From every vantage point in Thessalonica, Mount Olympus looms large on the southwest horizon. The Greeks believed that their great gods held court on its summit. Like many Mediterranean societies, the Thessalonians of Paul's day offered worship to an array of Greek, Roman, and even Egyptian gods. Uniquely, the city was dedicated to the Phrygian gods, the Cabeiri, whose mystery religion included drunken reveries and orgies. Layered onto all this was the required civil homage to the Roman Caesar.[3]

Into this polytheistic soup, Paul and his friends brought the good news of Jesus. Turning to Christ would require turning from the dominant religious culture. At least this would have been true for the bulk of the non-Jews of the city. However, not all the people shared the belief that the gods were many, as we learn from Luke's account in Acts 17.

- *When Paul and Silas came to Thessalonica, whom did they first approach with the good news? And what religious connections did they exploit to preach the gospel (17:1–4)?*

- *What was the thrust of Paul's message in the synagogue? How did he make his case to the Jews and God-fearers there?*

- *Why do you think Paul and Silas had a more receptive audience in Thessalonica than in Philippi?*

In Thessalonica, Paul began teaching to what might have been a receptive audience: Jews and Greek converts to Judaism. These were knowledgeable of the Hebrew Scriptures, submissive to the living God, and prepared for the coming Messiah. Paul proclaimed that Jesus was this promised Messiah. If this were true, then it was good news indeed!

Still bearing the bruises and wounds of his beating in Philippi, Paul also insisted that the Messiah had to suffer (v. 3). This statement was a major sticking point for observant Jews, as it is still today. The Messiah must rule, of course. He must conquer. He must lead. But suffer? This was not expected of the Messiah, so this notion demanded explanation and proof.

The Scriptures are clear, however. The coming Christ *was* appointed to suffer. The first-century Jewish community had not explored these prophecies as deeply as they did those about the victorious Christ, the defender Christ, the warrior Christ, or the anointed King. But these overlooked prophecies were in their Scriptures nonetheless.

Furthermore, as if a suffering Messiah wasn't enough, Paul taught that the Messiah had to rise from the dead (v. 3). Rising from the dead is a two-step process. The second step cannot happen without the first step, namely death. This would have come as a complete shock to Paul's Jewish audience. How could the long-awaited Messiah die?

This is why Jesus' own disciples could never take it in when Jesus spoke to them about his suffering and death. They refused to believe it. They resisted it. In fact, over Jesus' multiple attempts to explain it, they never clued in. It was too strange, too impossible, too un-Messiah-like.

- *Look up the following passages where Jesus talks with his disciples about his impending suffering, death, and resurrection. Then summarize their response to his revelation about his last days on earth.*

  *Matthew 16:21–22*

  *Matthew 17:22–23*

*Mark 8:31–32*

*Mark 9:9–10*

*Mark 9:31–32*

Through three successive weekly teaching sessions, Paul *proved* these unexpected truths to his Jewish and God-fearing audience. Paul used what we call the Old Testament to make his case to the Thessalonians, and he convinced a substantial number (Acts 17:1–4).

What Hebrew Scriptures did Paul refer to in his arguments for Messiah Jesus? Specifically, what passages promised that the Christ would suffer and die before his exaltation? We don't know for certain, but there is no shortage of Old Testament promises to that effect. From the first conversation after man's fall in the garden, the promised Savior was promised suffering.

• *Look up the following passages and note the hardship Jewish believers should have expected for their Christ.*

| | What suffering was promised for the Messiah? |
|---|---|
| *Genesis 3:15* | |
| *Psalm 22:6–8* | |
| *Psalm 22:16–18* | |
| *Psalm 41:9* | |
| *Psalm 69:19–21* | |
| *Isaiah 52:13–15* | |
| *Isaiah 53:2–3* | |
| *Isaiah 53:4–6* | |
| *Isaiah 53:7–9* | |
| *Isaiah 53:10–12* | |

## The Rise of Persecution

Among the Thessalonians that Paul persuaded was a prominent man named Jason, who offered his hospitality to Paul and company. We do not know whether Jason was Jewish or a gentile convert. His name was certainly Greek (think Jason and the Argonauts), but Jews living among Greeks would often Hellenize their names. Jason may have been born a Joshua.[4]

Either way, it is worth noting the short-term "reward" that Jason received for his faith in Christ and the support of these Christian missionaries. If he were Jewish, devout Jews would have hated him for trusting in the Messiah they rejected. If he were Greek, the non-Jewish citizens of the city would have resented him for rejecting the local religion and challenging the civic order through allegiance to another Lord—a Lord who stood above all other so-called lords. The Thessalonians suffered for their faith from the start.

- *What opposition did Paul face for his ministry in Thessalonica (Acts 17:5)? What motivated his enemies?*

- *What tactics and claims did these opponents use to pressure the Christians (vv. 6–9)?*

- *After sunset, what did the local believers do for Paul and Silas (v. 10)?*

- *Estimate the amount of time the apostles spent in Thessalonica. Based on this short account of Paul's time with them and the discipleship opportunities, would you describe the new community of believers as mature or immature? Strong or feeble? Stable or vulnerable?*

Wherever Paul preached Jesus' good news, some Jews opposed him. To Paul, this would have been no surprise. After all, this was exactly his own posture before the Lord Jesus met him on the road to Damascus. He was doing all he could to stop the message from getting out. He was pursuing and persecuting all who proclaimed it (Acts 26:9–18). He expected that other Jews would react the same way to him after his conversion.

On his first mission among the Galatians, Paul was opposed by Jews in the synagogue of Pisidian Antioch (13:44–52). And he was also persecuted by gentiles who joined the Jews in their hostilities (14:5, 19 –20). This theme of collusion between Jews and gentiles to oppose the gospel runs throughout the book of Acts.

In Thessalonica, this cross-cultural opposition resulted in a mob of thugs. When the mob could not find Paul and his companions, Jason and his companions faced the consequences. They were dragged before the city officials,[5] accused of disloyalty to Caesar, and forced to post a bond (probably guaranteeing that Paul and company would leave and not revisit the city).

The abbreviated account in Acts seems to imply that Paul stayed in Thessalonica for less than a month (most likely in the year 50[6]). Maybe so, but Philippians 4:16 indicates that he was there long enough to receive multiple support gifts from the young believers in Philippi.

The Thessalonian church was not obliterated as their enemies had hoped. Only Paul and his associates were uprooted from their effective ministry there. With their hurried departure, they could not know whether these new Christians were flourishing or withering under pressure. The question of the Thessalonians thriving in Christ, or even surviving, weighed heavily on the missionaries' hearts.

## DIGGING DEEPER

Paul's divine vision calling him to Macedonia led to the first intentional apostolic mission among the gentiles of Europe. In terms of strategy, response, and persecution, the Acts 16–17 account of the first three cities shows us surprising similarities and differences.

- *Skim through the passages about each place. Take special note of the different strategies Paul used and the people who received and rejected the gospel. Give your own brief assessment of the impact of their ministry as they traveled on, leaving churches where none had been before.*

| | **Philippi** (Acts 16:11–40) | **Thessalonica** (Acts 17:1–9) | **Berea** (Acts 17:10–15) |
|---|---|---|---|
| *Where did Paul initiate ministry in the city?* | | | |
| *How does Acts describe the early response there?* | | | |
| *Who opposed the gospel ministry?* | | | |
| *How did the believers respond to this resistance?* | | | |
| *Describe the state of the fledgling church in this city when Paul moved on.* | | | |

- *Recall how you first heard the good news of Jesus. Who gave you the news? What were the circumstances? How readily or reluctantly did you believe?*

- *As in Jason's case, choosing to follow Jesus can lead to immediate hardship. What opposition have you received for your faith in Christ? Has it been overt or subtle? Take comfort in Paul's assurance that "all who choose to live godly as worshipers of Jesus, the Anointed One, will also experience persecution" (2 Timothy 3:12).*

- *Think of someone you know who is new to the Christian faith. What can you share with that person to prepare him or her for difficulties sure to come?*

- *Our instinct is to withdraw from people who wrong or threaten us. Jesus calls his followers to resist that instinct. Read Luke 6:32–36. Consider how believers should respond to those who oppose us. Jot down some of your thoughts here, then keep them in mind the next time you face opposition because of your faith in Christ.*

# Talking It Out

Since Christians grow in community, not just in solitude, every "Talking It Out" section contains questions you may want to discuss with another person or in a group. Here are the exercises for this lesson.

1. Discuss with a small group how sharing Christ with these different groups of people requires different tactics: secular college students, Muslim immigrants, scientists, athletes, and former churchgoers.

2. Have each member of your group describe the sort of Christian leader they would be willing to suffer alongside. Have you ever known a person like that? Tell the group about them.

LESSON 2

# Show and Tell

(1 Thessalonians 1:1–10)

For many American schoolchildren, their first experience of public speaking is show-and-tell. The teacher asks the child to bring an object, a photo, or a house pet to class to show the other children. Then, while everyone is looking at the attraction, the child must talk about it, answering such questions as, *Why is this item special? Who gave it to you? What can you do with it? Who are the people in that photo? Where was it taken? What are they doing in that police car? What is Snuffy's favorite food? Why isn't she awake right now?*

Think of how awkward and confusing this exercise might be if it were only show—if the child put the object on the table but didn't explain its significance. The class would have to guess what it is or its importance. Just as bad would be if it were only tell. Without anything to look at, the class could conclude that the speaker is just making stuff up. Together, though, show-and-tell is effective. There is something interesting to look at and something to learn about it. Or something interesting to tell and a visual to reinforce it.

Communicating the Christian gospel needs to resemble show-and-tell. Some Christians specialize in the show part. They try to live good lives that serve as an example of the gospel. They go to church, volunteer in the community, and strive to be honest. They hope their religious niceness will win people over, but without a clear explanation, observers can only conclude that these are darn-good neighbors. Other Christians specialize in tell. They speak about the good news, sharing it with everyone they can. They tell and tell and tell. Secular people hear what they are saying, but they have difficulty squaring the words with the lives of the people doing the telling.

We need both the showing and the telling. We need a clear and coherent message that our lives confirm and recommend. Today's Christians don't always understand this, but the first-century Thessalonians did. We can see how well they understood the gospel from Paul's warm greeting to this new Christian community.

- *Who wrote this letter, remembering that first-century letters began with their authors (1 Thessalonians 1:1)?*

- *To whom was the letter written, and what was their relationship to the divine (v. 1)?*

- *From the outset of this letter, what evidence did Paul have of the Thessalonians' life in Christ? What motivated their Christian work and perseverance (vv. 2–3)?*

## DIGGING DEEPER

Many weddings include the reading from 1 Corinthians 13:13, which ends, "There are three things that remain: faith, hope, and love," but Paul's letter to the Thessalonians begins by mentioning these highest virtues. The fruit of their life in Jesus was grounded in and growing from these three. In essence, Paul told them that Christian faith works, Christian love labors, and Christian hope endures.

The combination of faith, hope, and love can be found throughout the New Testament. Whenever the Holy Spirit does his work of regeneration, the born-again soul begins to exhibit these precious qualities in increasing measure.

- *Look up the following passages and mark which of these three—faith, hope, or love—is mentioned. Then make note of how one virtue interacts with others for the Christian.*[7]

| Passage | Faith | Hope | Love | Interaction of these virtues |
|---|---|---|---|---|
| *Romans 5:5* | ❍ | ❍ | ❍ | |
| *1 Corinthians 13:12–13* | ❍ | ❍ | ❍ | |
| *Galatians 5:5–6* | ❍ | ❍ | ❍ | |
| *Ephesians 3:16–19* | ❍ | ❍ | ❍ | |
| *Colossians 1:3–6* | ❍ | ❍ | ❍ | |
| *1 Thessalonians 1:3* | ❍ | ❍ | ❍ | |
| *1 Thessalonians 5:8* | ❍ | ❍ | ❍ | |
| *2 Thessalonians 2:16–17* | ❍ | ❍ | ❍ | |
| *1 Timothy 4:10–12* | ❍ | ❍ | ❍ | |
| *Philemon 1:4–6* | ❍ | ❍ | ❍ | |
| *Hebrews 11:1* | ❍ | ❍ | ❍ | |
| *1 Peter 1:21–22* | ❍ | ❍ | ❍ | |

## The Gospel Received

- *How did Paul describe the way the good news was initially delivered in Thessalonica (1 Thessalonians 1:4–5)? What added punch to the message? What was the show for Paul's tell?*

- *Why was Paul confident of the Thessalonians' conversion to faith in Christ? Whose example did they imitate? What harsh reality was part of the examples the Thessalonians followed (vv. 6–7)?*

When teaching most practical skills, we know how important visuals are. Imagine explaining over the phone how to tie a shoelace: "Cross the right-hand string over the left-hand string. Then loop the right-hand string back under the left-hand string. Now, pull it tight." In that single instruction, it is easy to see the confusion that might result. And we are not even halfway finished. Even if this instruction makes sense to the hearer, it is because she can picture it in her mind due to having seen someone do it before. When we were young, someone modeled this explanation for us until we could understand and learn to do it ourselves *and* eventually model it again for others.

This is how we learn to tie our shoes, brush our teeth, write our alphabet, boil an egg, and a myriad of other everyday skills. Why do we think we need show-and-tell for the mundane abilities of life but that we can understand the Christian message and the life it inspires just by reading a book or listening to a sermon? Paul did not believe this. Neither did Jesus.

After his baptism and wilderness temptation, Jesus began his ministry by calling a small group of followers to his side. Their first calling was to follow (Mark 1:16–20; 2:13–14), simply to be with him (3:13–15). Then they could witness the life of God the Son directly, seeing what he was like, hearing what he taught, and watching what he did. This eclectic little group of disciples would spend at least three years with Jesus.[8] And when it was time for them to lead his movement, they would be like their Master, saying what he said and doing what he did.

Paul was not in Thessalonica for long, but he was there long enough. In his short tenure, he clearly taught the simple gospel while showing the people the gospel-transformed life. He showed and told them that living for Jesus was worth any suffering that might come as a result. He showed and told them how to work hard as believers without burdening anyone else. He showed and told them how to confidently speak out about Jesus in the face of opposition. It was this show-and-tell that they responded to. It was this model and message that changed their lives.

- *After the Thessalonians learned the gospel and gospel living from Paul and his companions, what new role did these believers play in the Jesus movement (1 Thessalonians 1:7–8)? What influence did they have on the lives of others? How far-reaching was their influence?*

- *What kind of reputation did the Thessalonian Christians have in the region? What news about them got back to Paul (vv. 9–10)?*

After Paul and his friends were uprooted by the riot in Thessalonica, they moved on to Berea and Athens before settling in Corinth for a year and a half (Acts 18:11). Most Bible scholars think that Paul wrote his first letter to the Thessalonians during that period in Corinth, the capital city of Achaia. Word about the faith and example of the Thessalonians gradually filtered back to Paul while he waited and prayed for them. They had an impact in their own province of Macedonia, but their exemplary faith also influenced people in Achaia, the adjacent province.

These new believers followed Paul's Christian model until they became model Christians. Their lives set an example for all the people of their region in southern Greece. Their admirable faith showed others the way to Jesus. One might conclude that they specialized in showing the gospel.

Many modern Christians have advocated for what the sociologist and priest Andrew Greeley called "the evangelism of a good example."[9] They believe that a faithful life will entice people to seek out the truth about the nature of God, the human sin dilemma, and God's good news of salvation. Without a persuasive verbal explanation, people will intuit their need and God's solution. Or, at the very least, they will be drawn to the religious services of the Christians' good example and want to hear more about these things. These advocates will blithely quote the maxim attributed to St. Francis of Assisi, "Preach the gospel at all times; when necessary, use words."[10]

Jesus never intended his disciples to quietly, subtly, wordlessly behave well enough for others to join the faith. Obviously, neither did Paul. Remember, he arrived in Thessalonica with the bruises he earned with his words. His life example included proclaiming the message of Jesus, even to the point of suffering.

It is this show-and-tell example that the Thessalonians followed. While they lived Jesus-transformed lives, they declared his good news loudly and boldly. It "sounded out" from them all over their region (1 Thessalonians 1:8). An expanding audience heard the good news from their lips just like the Thessalonians had heard it from Paul. The imitators became the imitated.

## WORD WEALTH

Paul called the Thessalonians "an example" for others throughout the region (v. 7). The Greek word translated "example" is *typos*. It usually describes a stamp or the impression made by a stamp. It is where we get our English word *type*, as in typesetting and typecasting, the lasting impression made by a tool or an experience.[11]

When the apostle Thomas refused to believe Christ had risen unless he saw the imprint from the nails in Jesus' hands, he used the word *typos*. Old Testament figures are also called "types" as they set either a good or bad template for believers to become (Acts 7:44; Romans 5:12–14; 1 Corinthians 10:1–6; Hebrews 8:5). The most common use, of course, is the example set by the apostles and their ministry (Romans 6:17; Philippians 3:17; 2 Thessalonians 3:9; 1 Timothy 4:12; Titus 2:7; 1 Peter 5:3).

Here, the Thessalonian believers have been stamped by the apostles, and now their lives are leaving a permanent spiritual impression on others.

## A Personal Testimony of Faith

- *Besides the good news message that sounded out from them, what other details about the Thessalonians' conversion became public knowledge (1 Thessalonians 1:9)? What major changes took place in them after they heard the gospel?*

- *What future event became the Thessalonian hope (v. 10)? How would this focus sustain them through the hardships of following Christ?*

A personal conversion story is a powerful tool in evangelism. Every believer has one. Usually, our story will include what we were like before Jesus, how we came to believe in Jesus, and how our lives have changed as a result. Sometimes we call this a person's testimony.

The apostles used their personal testimonies to proclaim the gospel. On two occasions in Acts, Paul recounted his Damascus Road conversion while explaining the gospel (Acts 22:3–21; 26:2–29). Peter recalled his experience on the Mount of Transfiguration to undergird his message as an eyewitness (2 Peter 1:16–18). Similarly, John reminded his readers that he was only telling them what he himself learned firsthand.

> We saw him with our very own eyes. We gazed upon him and heard him speak. Our hands actually touched him, the one who was from the beginning, the Living Expression of God. This Life-Giver was made visible and we have seen him. We testify to this truth: the eternal Life-Giver lived face-to-face with the Father and has now dawned upon us. So we proclaim to you what we have seen and heard about this Life-Giver so that we may share and enjoy this life together. (1 John 1:1–3)

One of the Bible's most compelling testimonies, however, comes from a nameless follower of Christ (John 9:1–38). After the man endured a life of blindness, Jesus healed him. When Jesus' enemies demanded an explanation for the miracle and a defense of Jesus' character and ministry, the exasperated man simply answered, "I have no idea what kind of man he is. All I know is that I was blind and now I can see for the first time in my life!" (v. 25).

Testimonies can be persuasive all on their own. They show the power of the gospel to change lives. They show that the message is not only propositional; it is also personal, emotional, even dramatic. Furthermore, faith testimonies have the added benefit of being inarguable. Others can object to facts, they can rebut some arguments, but they cannot deny someone else's experiences.

Obviously, the Thessalonians proclaimed the message they had received through the retelling of their own conversion stories. The Greeks knew the Thessalonian story. They had heard about their welcome reception of the good news, their previous devotion to false pagan gods, and their radical turnaround to embrace the truth of Jesus. They heard about the Thessalonians' change of mind, change of life, and change of hope.

This show-and-tell is the Lord's plan to reach the world. When Jesus met with his followers one last time before his ascension, he gave them an enormous task. The first generation of believers received a multi-generational mission (Matthew 28:17–20). In fact, it would take them an entire epoch to get it done. All the nations had to hear Jesus' good news. People from everywhere had to be baptized in the name of the Father, Son, and Holy Spirit. They had to teach every people group the things that Jesus taught them.

The disciples would become disciple-makers. And their disciples would become disciple-makers. And their disciples and their disciples and their disciples...until now, when some disciple-maker made a disciple of you.

## EXPERIENCE GOD'S HEART

- *In expressing your Christian faith, have you leaned toward show or tell? Is your church or denomination inclined one way or the other? What would have to change for your approach to show and tell the gospel?*

- *If you can, contact one of the people who influenced you to follow Christ. To get a perspective on the generational mission of the gospel, ask this individual to tell you their personal testimony. Then thank them for their impact on your life, especially if they showed and told you how to follow Jesus.*

# SHARE GOD'S HEART

- *Write out your personal testimony. In the first paragraph or two, describe your life before you trusted in Christ. The next portion should explain the circumstances of when you first heard the good news and your response. Were you eager to hear it or resistant? Did you go through a long process to faith? Describe what persuaded you. Then, in the last paragraphs, describe what is different about your life and worldview now.*

- *Make a short list of the people who should hear or read your personal testimony. Pray for an opportunity to share your story with them.*

# Talking It Out

1. Discuss the hazards of showing the gospel without telling it and telling the gospel without showing it. What damage can be done when one or the other is neglected when we try to communicate Jesus' message to others?

2. Talk about the areas of discipleship where you feel you lacked a model to show you how to live in Christ. For example, did anyone model prayer, Scripture meditation, or evangelism for you? It isn't too late. Good examples are out there. Suggest ways to find someone who can teach you by example.

LESSON 3

# A Measure of Ministry

## (1 Thessalonians 2:1–16)

We have considered the importance of showing the gospel while telling the gospel. A transformed Christian makes a powerful case for a new life in Christ. The testimony of how that change came about can show others their own way to faith.

Everyone knows, however, that not every Christian example is helpful to the reputation of the good news of Jesus. With little difficulty, most contemporary non-believers can point to a bevy of bad examples: an abusive priest, a disgraced faith healer, a greedy televangelist, an authoritarian pastor, a scandal-ridden conference speaker. Religious inconsistency, greed, compromise, insincerity, or scandal do great damage.

The good can be lumped in with the bad. The corrupt representatives of the Lord can undermine people's opinion of the Lord himself. Deeply flawed messengers can hinder the message. Famous phonies damage not only their own ministry but also the reception of other messengers who are trying to proclaim the truth. This means that faithful evangelists and Bible teachers must dismantle suspicion before they can effectively spread the faith.

The Thessalonian believers knew that Paul's influence in their city was exceedingly good, but not everyone was convinced. Remember, the opposition went so far as to start a destructive riot to be rid of him. From their point of view, Paul swept into town challenging the Jewish conception of the Messiah, denying the legitimacy of the indigenous religion, and threatening allegiance to Caesar. Then, when confronted, Paul went into hiding and sneaked away into the night, leaving behind confused new converts.

In his absence, only that new community of faith could counter this narrative. Paul was eager to help them make that case. In the next portion of Paul's letter, he defended his ministry against accusations like these. Because of his gospel show-and-tell, he appealed to their own experiences with him when he lived among them.

- *Review 1 Thessalonians 1:2–2:1. What evidence did the Thessalonians have to show that Paul's ministry there was fruitful?*

- *What risk did Paul take in preaching the good news to them? What experiences might have made him and his companions reluctant to carry on a ministry in Thessalonica?*

- *Paul listed ten things that were not true of his ministry (1:1–9). See if you can list at least five of them.*

- *What was his purpose in listing the negative qualities missing from his example and preaching?*

- *Are these descriptions applicable to some Christian ministries today? Which ones come to mind?*

- *In contrast, Paul also listed nine things that were true of his gospel work among the Thessalonians (vv. 2–12). Again, can you note at least five of them? Would an evangelist or church-planter today want to be described in the same way? What aspects might be different in our modern culture?*

Paul reminded his readers that his ministry among them was good in every way. Of particular interest are the invisible qualities Paul listed, such as his motives, his sincerity, and his desire to please only God. He noted that only God can test the heart, but he was so confident of his own righteousness that he was unafraid to appeal to God's approval.

In Paul's estimation, all the accusations against him and his friends were false. On the contrary, their example should be our standard for all gospel ministries. It certainly became the measure of ministry for this young Thessalonian church.

- *In what practical ways did Paul demonstrate a greed-free ministry (vv. 8–9)? What hardship would this approach have created for Paul?*

- *Was "tentmaking" a requirement for gospel ministry? Explain your answer.*

We know from Acts 18:3 that when Paul settled in Corinth, he was a tentmaker by trade. This skill proved invaluable to him while he was awaiting the arrival of his colleagues, Silas and Timothy. Paul's letter to the Thessalonians indicates that he also plied his trade while he was among them. He worked hard to pay his own way in order to avoid being a burden to the new Christians.

Many missionaries and ministers today take inspiration from Paul's tentmaking example. This is especially so when spearheading gospel ministry into new communities or revitalizing churches in decline. Without a base of mature Christians to give generously to support the ministry, a Christian worker might provide for his own needs through another job. In many countries where visas are routinely denied to Christian workers, missionaries will often assume other jobs (e.g., doctor, nurse, architect, construction, food distributor) to gain gospel access with a work visa.

Is "tentmaking" God's preferred approach to missions? Elsewhere, Paul argued that he had a right to financial support but that he yielded that right for the sake of the gospel (1 Corinthians 9:11–14). The Thessalonian and Corinthian Christians obviously benefited materially from Paul's generous sacrificial labors. Surely, this would also be true in any modern ministry context. Some have argued for "tentmaking" to be the norm,[12] but it is instructive that when Silas and Timothy did arrive, Paul dedicated himself full-time to preaching and defending the good news (Acts 18:5). It is clear, however, that tentmaking protected Paul from the charge of fleecing the people of Thessalonica.

## Family Portrait

- *What family relationships did Paul use to describe his demeanor while he worked among the Thessalonians (1 Thessalonians 2:1, 7–8, 11, 14)?*

- *What insights do each of these family roles teach us about life in the family of God?*

When a company holds a big event for families, like a picnic, a day at the amusement park, a concert, or a banquet, they often hire a photographer. That professional must capture the spirit of the day on film. They should portray employees and their loved ones having fun, relaxing with colleagues, chatting happily together, and enjoying food. They need to show that the business is more than profit and loss, marketing and manufacturing. Their company is one big, happy family.

The company newsletter or the corporate social media platforms will feature those photos. The minute they are posted, all the employees will scour the gallery for the faces of their own family members. The management may see a company family event; the workers see their families at a company event.

In Thessalonians 2, we see snapshots taken from the apostle's ministry days in their city and, in them, all the members of the family of God in Paul and company. He calls himself their sibling, the baby, the mother, and the father in the family as he recalls their time together.

The most common collective noun for other Christians in the New Testament epistles is brothers (or brothers and sisters).[13] Over a hundred times, the apostles use these terms in their letters. For Jesus' earliest hand-selected apostles to call new converts their siblings shows humility as well as theological accuracy. As Paul wrote here, he and his coworkers could have asserted their spiritual authority, but they seldom did. They saw themselves on a level with all of God's children, adopted by the same grace into the same family. They had a special role in Jesus' kingdom, but their status in the family was the same as it was for other brothers and sisters in Christ.[14]

Besides the sibling status, Paul considered himself their spiritual parent in both the maternal and paternal roles. The tender care that a baby requires from its mother reminded Paul of the tenderness he felt for them. His self-sacrificial motherly love for them led him to stay up late and work all day for their benefit while nurturing them as they took their first steps of faith.

And, finally, like a wise and engaged father, Paul gave them the steadiness and direction they needed to grow up quickly in the Lord. He taught them the truth and supported them as they began to walk confidently in their new faith. He coached them to embrace fully the Christian life and message, pushing them to keep going.

## DIGGING DEEPER

In the Bible, the church was organic. It was never a physical meeting space. It was a subset of human beings, specifically, the followers of Jesus called out from the rest of humanity. Even the word pictures used to describe it are living things: seed sown in a field, yeast working through the dough, a grapevine, a body, a flock, and so on.

Perhaps the most common way to talk about the Christian church is as a family. Believers are children of God the Father, brothers and sisters in Christ.

- *Look up the passages below to see just a smattering of the references to the family of God. Sometimes the whole family is referenced and sometimes only specific family members. Place in the chart that follows each Scripture reference under the family member mentioned. Some passages will fall into more than one column.*

  Matthew 18:1–4

  Mark 3:31–35

  John 1:10–13

  Romans 8:15–17

  1 Corinthians 3:1–2

  Galatians 4:4–6

  Galatians 6:9–10

  Ephesians 3:14–15

  1 Thessalonians 4:9–10

  1 Timothy 5:1–2

  Hebrews 2:10–15

  1 Peter 1:13–17

  1 Peter 2:2–3

  1 John 2:12–14

  1 John 3:1–3

| Whole Family | Baby | Father | Mother | Children |
|---|---|---|---|---|
| | | | | |

## Good Results from Good Work

- *To conclude his defense, Paul circled back to his initial point. Their sowing and cultivation of the spiritual fields in Thessalonica had produced a good crop. The proof of good methods was in the product.*

- *What did the Thessalonians think was the source of Paul's teaching (1 Thessalonians 2:13)? When Paul had to leave them swiftly, what confidence did he have that his teaching would continue to have a good effect?*

- *What experience did the Thessalonians have in common with the Jewish Christians living near Jerusalem (vv. 14–15)? How had the Jewish leaders treated the Jewish Messiah and his followers? How had the Greek leaders treated followers of Jesus in Thessalonica?*

- *What motive did Paul ascribe to the Jewish opposition that followed him wherever he went (v. 15–16)? Why did they want to hinder gentiles from following Jesus?*

- *How do we know that Paul's condemnation of "the Jews" here was not anti-Semitic?*

*What do you think it means that these enemies were "filling up to the brim the measure of their guilt" (v. 16)?*

Because Paul was teaching God's Word and not his own, he could expect God to continue working in the hearts of these new converts even when Paul was whisked away. The situation was not ideal, and, as we will soon see, it gave him great concern, but the way the Thessalonians accepted Paul's word as God's Word gave him great hope.

Even though Paul left them in the middle of persecution, he also saw this as proof of their genuine faith. Like all the believers from the start of the Jesus movement, they were facing the expected consequences of following the Savior. It was no different for the gentiles than it had been for Jews. National and religious loyalties are always challenged when people give their allegiance to Jesus above all else.

Paul was a Jewish persecutor before he was a Jewish Christian. As a convert himself, he remained Jewish, but he was brokenhearted and frustrated by those who defended his old mindset. It was not enough that they rejected their own Messiah; they were determined to keep others from believing in him too. Especially, they were incensed that anyone claiming to be the Jewish Messiah also came to save gentiles.

Paul no longer had patience for this thinking. In his denunciation in 1 Thessalonians, he echoed the woes that Jesus himself pronounced against the unbelieving Jewish leaders opposing him: "Great sorrow awaits you religious scholars and you Pharisees—such frauds and pretenders! You do all you can to keep people from experiencing the reality of heaven's kingdom realm. Not only do you refuse to enter in, you also forbid anyone else from entering in!" (Matthew 23:13).

A bad witness can do a lot of damage to the good news, but in his ministry among the Thessalonians, Paul and his companions had nothing to be ashamed of. Their ministry was a good witness for the good news of Jesus and a measure for other ministries. Theirs was a good message delivered with good methods springing from good motives and accomplishing good results.

## EXPERIENCE GOD'S HEART

- *Read through the list of Paul's denials (1 Thessalonians 2:1–6). If any of these things had been true of Paul, how would it have affected his credibility?*

- *Is there anything in your character that could make it hard for others to follow Christ? If so, what is it?*

- *Now reread the way Paul described their work (vv. 7–12). Can you see how character like that supports spreading the message of Christ? Explain your answer.*

- *Is there anything in your character that would make following Jesus attractive? If so, what is it?*

Go before the Lord and lay your character before him. Ask him, through his Spirit, to work in you to further transform your character so it mirrors Christ's more clearly and serves to attract more people to him.

## SHARE GOD'S HEART

- *Some of the people you know have been wounded by a ministry conducted in a way contrary to the gospel. Consider asking them to recall that story for you. Resist the urge to be defensive and simply listen to their experience. Afterward, pray for them. And if you hear anything that leads you to wince in your soul, to see some damage that you and your witness may have caused, ask the Lord to mitigate and overcome that damage and show you how you can be more effective for him in the future.*

- *Maybe you were wounded by someone who behaved in a way contrary to the gospel. How did you persevere in faith or come back around to believe? What keys did you find in dealing with Christian hypocrisy that others might need to hear?*

# Talking It Out

1. Paul described himself as a brother, a baby, a mother, and a father. Talk about how each of these metaphors is helpful in setting an example for other Christians. Share with one another which ones best describe you.

2. How could the modern church benefit from using Paul's standards for evaluating ministries? If we applied his description of the character and methods of that first missionary team, how do you think our contemporaries might measure up? What pitfalls could we avoid?

LESSON 4

# Absence Makes the Heart to Wonder

(1 Thessalonians 2:17–3:5)

The church-planter felt his work was complete. For more than a decade, he had worked to establish a solid gospel-centered church. The church was now paying its bills, making its own decisions, and sending out workers. They had mature leadership and supported worldwide and local missions. They were engaged in practical ministry and had a good reputation in the community. They even had a building of their own. It was time to move on to carry out some other groundbreaking work elsewhere, but what would become of this body of believers after their founding pastor moved away?

Christian parents drop off their beloved daughter at the dormitory of a state university known for its carousing. They have done their best to prepare her for the temptations and challenges of university life. They have researched the campus ministries and local churches to help her form a supportive network of believers. Now they must return home and hope that she will thrive in her studies and in the Lord.

A church sent out a mission team overseas for ministry alongside a missionary in a remote place. While they enjoyed safe and uneventful travel to the field and initial reports of ministry were good, communications ceased after the first two days. Probably, the church members assured themselves, this was only due to technology rather than something dangerous. Still, there was no way to know for sure.

We cannot control all the situations in our own lives, let alone those of the people we love. No matter how much we want to help them, no matter what we would change if we could, there are times when we are helpless. Sometimes it seems that all we can do is look on from a distance while health scares, sinful temptation, physical danger, or relationship breakdowns throw lives into turmoil. It seems that way, but there is one thing we can do: we can pray.

Paul was in this situation with the new Christians at Thessalonica. There is an old saying that "Absence makes the heart to wander," suggesting that physical distance produces distance in the relationship. For Paul, this could not be more wrong. Absence only made him think more often of these new believers and wonder.

He had no control over the riot that had uprooted him from their city.

He had no control over the way Jewish opponents and their gentile collaborators persecuted the believers he left behind.

He had no idea what other difficulties these Christians had to endure in his absence.

- *He could only wonder how they would do under the strain. And he could pray.*

- *What violent imagery did Paul use to describe his physical separation from the Thessalonians (1 Thessalonians 2:17–18)? How did he describe his longing to be with them again? What was blocking that desire from being fulfilled?*

- *How did Paul describe the Thessalonian believers who became the source of his "glorious pride and joy" (vv. 19–20)?*

The more we love someone, the more their well-being matters to us. If we were to hear that a successful political coup has happened somewhere in the world, overthrowing a tyrant and paving the way for freedom, we might be intrigued. But if we were political refugees from that country, we would be overjoyed. When we learn of a cure for a particular cancer, we might be glad to hear about it. But if it is our child suffering from that cancer, we would be overjoyed.

Paul and his companions were driven away from these new followers of Christ, their own spiritual offspring. They loved them and longed for them. They treasured them and exulted in them. The Thessalonians' spiritual well-being was of utmost personal importance to Paul. He was not a disinterested observer who could be contented with whatever news might come. Only the spiritual thriving of the Thessalonians would satisfy the longings of the apostle. He had to know.

- *Where was Paul when he could no longer bear the suspense (3:1–2)? How many stops beyond Thessalonica was that (Acts 17:10–16)?*

- *Which of the authors of this letter (1 Thessalonians 1:1) was sent to check up on the Thessalonian Christians (3:2)? With what complimentary terms did Paul describe this colleague?*

- *What did they hope would result from Timothy returning to them?*

- *What specific threats was Paul concerned about (3:3–5)? What hard reality did he call the Christian's destiny? How does that certainty strike you? Does it match your experience?*

Timothy was free to return to Thessalonica, but Paul was not. In 1 Thessalonians 2:18, Paul described this restriction as spiritual opposition, but this was probably his insightful interpretation of the practical facts. Perhaps the bond that Jason agreed to (Acts 17:9) prohibited Paul and maybe Silas from returning. Maybe Timothy's gentile cultural identity was less likely to arouse interest or opposition. Whatever the cause, the missionaries thought it was wise to send only the youngest member of their team back for an update.

Timothy was in no way a second-string player on this team. Paul called him a trusted colleague, as active in spreading the gospel as Paul himself was. He was confident of Timothy's abilities to make the Thessalonians stronger, more courageous and faithful, and less intimidated by persecution.

## The Unwelcome Promise

Many of the promises of God are comforting, even triumphant. For example, our strength will be renewed when we trust him (Isaiah 40:31). His peace will fill us when we release our anxieties to him (Philippians 4:4–6). He directs the circumstances of our lives for our good when we love him (Romans 8:28). By faith, all his people will overcome the world (1 John 5:4). Ultimately, even death will be defeated because of the resurrection of Jesus (1 Corinthians 15:54–57). Believers long for the Lord to keep these promises.

But there is another biblical promise that we do not want him to keep. His followers will always suffer. We may never read these Scriptures in a verse-a-day calendar or on an inspirational poster, but they are abundant in the Bible nonetheless.

It should come as no surprise that the followers of Jesus, the Suffering Savior, will experience suffering of their own. The trajectory he set for us follows the arc of the cross. In fact, there is no following him without taking up our own cross (Mark 8:34–35). This simple, profound, unwelcome promise was part of Paul's teaching during his brief time among the Thessalonians. It prepared the new believers for the ongoing ordeal of the Christian life in a hostile, pagan world.

## DIGGING DEEPER

- *To get a feel for how extensive this teaching is in the New Testament, look up the following passages. Match the first portion of the verse with the second, putting in the blank the letter of the matching statement. (After you finish, feel free to check the endnote for the answers.[15]) Take special note of the verses around these that describe the purpose and results of promised hardship. We are not assured of a comfortable life in Jesus, but we are assured of a rewarding outcome.*

| **The verse starts like this...** | | **...and ends like this.** | |
|---|---|---|---|
| *Matthew 5:10* | How enriched you are when persecuted for doing what is right! | ____ | A. will also experience persecution. |

| | | | |
|---|---|---|---|
| *Matthew 10:22* | Expect to be hated by all because of my name, | _____ | B. And you must be willing to share my cross and experience it as your own. |
| *Matthew 16:24* | If you truly want to follow me, you should at once completely reject and disown your own life. | _____ | C. don't be bewildered as though something strange were overwhelming you. |
| *Luke 6:22* | How favored you become when you are hated, excommunicated, or slandered, | _____ | D. if you experience the world's hatred. |
| *John 15:18* | Just remember, when the unbelieving world hates you, | _____ | E. even when you endure hardships because of unjust suffering. |
| *Romans 5:3* | Even in times of trouble we have a joyful confidence, | _____ | F. but be faithful to the end and you will experience life and deliverance. |
| *Romans 8:17* | We will experience being co-glorified with him | _____ | G. For then you experience the realm of heaven's kingdom. |
| *2 Corinthians 1:7* | We know that just as you share in our sufferings | _____ | H. or when your name is spoken of as evil because of your love for me, the Son of Man. |

| | | | |
|---|---|---|---|
| *2 Timothy 3:12* | For all who choose to live godly as worshipers of Jesus, the Anointed One, | ____ | I. you are greatly blessed, because the Spirit of glory and power, who is the Spirit of God, rests upon you. |
| *James (Jacob) 1:12* | If your faith remains strong, even while surrounded by life's difficulties, | ____ | J. provided that we accept his sufferings as our own. |
| *1 Peter 2:19* | You find God's favor by deciding to please God | ____ | K. you will also share in God's comforting strength. |
| *1 Peter 4:12* | If life gets extremely difficult, with many tests, | ____ | L. you will continue to experience the untold blessings of God! |
| *1 Peter 4:14* | If you are insulted because of the name of Christ, | ____ | M. they first hated me. |
| *1 John 3:13* | So don't be shocked, beloved brothers and sisters, | ____ | N. knowing that our pressures will develop in us patient endurance. |

## Warning! Enemy Afoot

The same enemy that prevented Paul from revisiting their city was working to dissuade the Thessalonians from following Jesus. The apostle understood what many modern readers will overlook or dismiss. We have a real, personal, spiritual enemy who desires our downfall. Through temptation, discouragement, and even practical roadblocks to ministry, Satan works *hard* to stop the progress of God's life-saving mission.

Satan tormented righteous Job (Job 1:1–2:10). He hurled accusations at the high priest Joshua (Zechariah 3:1–5). He humiliated Peter (Luke 22:31–32). He even tried to distract and sideline Jesus (Matthew 4:1–11; 16:21–23). He is powerful, and his efforts are crafty and lethal. It is spiritual suicide to disregard him.

From personal experience, Peter described the deadly nature of his work: "Be well balanced and always alert, because your enemy, the devil, roams around incessantly, like a roaring lion looking for its prey to devour. Take a decisive stand against him and resist his every attack with strong, vigorous faith. For you know that your believing brothers and sisters around the world are experiencing the same kinds of troubles you endure" (1 Peter 5:8–9).

This ravenous, man-eating enemy goes after every believer incessantly. He will use all kinds of weapons and tactics to bring us down. He will destroy us if he can. His opposition would be terrifying if we had no means to fight back. Thankfully, we have an effective countermove.

Our simple and powerful response is to resist him by faith (1 John 4:4; 5:4–5). Paul told the Ephesian Christians that their faith could withstand all his attacks (Ephesians 6:16). Jesus' half-brother wrote that this simple act of standing firm would make the devil flee (James [Jacob] 4:7). This does not mean that Satan's tactics will cause us no suffering, but it does mean we are assured victory when we maintain our faith against his onslaught (Revelation 12:10–11).

Paul knew what these young Thessalonian believers were up against. He himself had been used by the tempter to oppose the church in its early days. Since his conversion, Paul had faced the brunt of the devil's attacks as he tried to forward the gospel (Acts 9:16). He was well acquainted with the hardships our enemy can bring against us. So naturally, he was concerned.

Take note, however, that the apostle Paul was most concerned that the Thessalonians' faith would endure. He was not worried about their health, their financial stability, their success, or their ease. He was worried that the tempter would lure them away from trusting fully in Jesus. Would the scorn of others or persecution from them discourage the Thessalonians from remaining faithful? Would their old religions recapture their hearts? Would worldly appetites entice them away from their holy calling? Would they grow dissatisfied with their newfound life in Christ? Would doubts about the gospel overwhelm them in the absence of their spiritual mentors? How would they survive? How could they, with such a new and fragile faith in the face of such cunning and effective opposition?

Until Timothy returned, Paul could only wonder about these things from a distance.

## EXPERIENCE GOD'S HEART

- *How do you feel when you think of Jesus' unwelcome promise of suffering for the believer? Are you frustrated that God would allow such things to come upon those who love him? Do you dread what may lie ahead? Or do you have confidence that whatever comes, it will be okay?*

- *How are you deepening your walk with Jesus in preparation for the next inevitable assault?*

- *Have you ever felt intense opposition from our enemy? Was it sinful temptation, discouragement, hostility from others, or practical obstacles? Did you think of it as a spiritual attack at the time? How did you do in those circumstances?*

## SHARE GOD'S HEART

- *A believer you know is probably experiencing a spiritual attack right now. They may have shared with you their struggle with sin or a spiritual defeat. Phone them to ask how they are holding up. If they will let you, pray aloud for them.*

- *Certainly, the missionaries you know are facing spiritual opposition. Our enemy does not like to lose any territory. Message the missionary you know through email or a messenger app and ask about spiritual warfare. You may get an education about the sorts of things those on the spiritual front lines have to face every day.*

# Talking It Out

1. Have you ever been in a situation where the well-being of someone you loved was outside your control and you could only hope from a distance that they would survive or perhaps even thrive? Share your experiences with each other.

2. Talk about how we can help each other resist the devil's attacks. What interactions might actually be harmful in our struggle? What would be an effective way to encourage one another?

LESSON 5

# Relieved by the Report

(1 Thessalonians 3:6–13)

Absence makes the heart to wonder. So how did things go for the newly established modern church after the founding church-planter moved away?

Despite their many strengths, the young church struggled. Different leadership brought different priorities and a different direction. Ministries were reorganized, and some were dropped altogether. Members who had been part of the congregation from the start felt sidelined and rejected. Sin was confronted. Conflict arose and simmered. The finances suffered. The mission budget was trimmed. Outreach efforts slowed. The congregation began to dissipate, beginning a downward spiral.

Within five years of the founding pastor's departure, the church that seemed so strong was no longer meeting together. The new pastor resigned and moved away. The building was sold to another local congregation, and most of the members drifted off to other churches. The worst fears of the broken-hearted church-planter had come to pass.

A result like this was what the apostle worried might become of the Thessalonians without the influence of his missionary team. He worried that spiritual attacks might render fruitless the ministry efforts there. So he waited with great anticipation for Timothy's return.

Spoiler alert. Since we have already read the first chapters, we know the basic content of the report. Paul wrote this whole letter after Timothy's return. Their efforts were not in vain. The Thessalonian church was doing great! Their flourishing was a delightful surprise, and Paul spent parts of 1 Thessalonians (1:2–10 and 2:13–16) rejoicing in it before he circled back to give this autobiographical context.

- *Paul was headed for Athens when he sent Timothy back to Thessalonica (1 Thessalonians 3:1). Where was Paul when Timothy returned, and what was Paul doing (Acts 18:1–5)?*

- *How did the Thessalonian Christians think of Paul and company (v. 6)?*

- *What made all of Paul's persecutions worth it (vv. 7–8)? What was the effect of their faithfulness on Paul? What caused him to feel fully alive?*

Timothy returned to Thessalonica to encourage the new Christians there. In fact, the new Christians encouraged him. When he brought good news back to Paul and the others about the flourishing new community, they were also buoyed in spirit despite their own ongoing hardships. This terrific news invigorated the uneasy missionaries. Who ministered to whom?

Sometimes our desperate prayers and longings are fulfilled in those we pray for from a distance. Not only do they survive, but they thrive in our absence. Their difficult circumstances produce spiritual growth that could not take place in an environment of ease and safety. When Paul and his friends were uprooted from Thessalonica, they hoped and prayed for just such a result. Timothy confirmed that their prayers were answered.

Paul's response to these answered prayers was more prayer.

- *What was Paul's first prayer instinct when he heard the fantastic news from Thessalonica (v. 9)?*

- *After Timothy had such an encouraging encounter with them, what did Paul begin to pray for in earnest (vv. 10–11)? What do you think he meant when he wrote that he could furnish what was lacking in their faith?*

As Paul poured out his thanksgiving, he prayed that God would allow him the same privilege that Timothy had. This was not a new desire (2:18). All along, he wanted the Lord to overcome Satan's hindrances so he could be face-to-face with the Thessalonian church. Knowing that they were flourishing was a relief, but now he wanted to see this miracle firsthand.

Paul longed for reunion because the church is an in-person phenomenon. Christians are meant to gather, to be face-to-face, to be physically present with one another. From the start of the Christian movement, believers gathered in person. At first, their meetings happened daily (Acts 2:46–47). Later, they met at least as often as once a week (1 Corinthians 16:2). By the writing of the letter to the Hebrews, some were neglecting these gatherings and had to be reminded of their importance (Hebrews 10:24–25). Many Christians need the same reminder today.

When God revealed himself most fully to us, he sent Jesus in the flesh (Hebrews 1:1–3). The incarnation brought God the Son face-to-face with his creatures. The flesh-and-blood Savior established a flesh-and-blood church. He even gave them a simple ritual meal to celebrate to remember his flesh and blood. We can only share in this remembrance when we are together.

Of course, we believe that the church of Jesus is made up of all the believers in the world, many of whom we will never meet in person. Furthermore, we believe that the church includes all the believers who have ever lived, even those who died before we were born. We acknowledge, therefore, that there is a spiritual reality to the church that is beyond physical presence, but we must not disregard the importance of being together. One day, every member of the church will gather to praise the Incarnate Lamb of God (Revelation 7:9–17). The spiritual church will have a physical reunion. Paul's prayers were the expression of the longing all God's people have for the face-to-face togetherness of that great reunion.

- *What spiritual trait did Paul desire in superabundance for the Thessalonian believers (1 Thessalonians 3:12)? To whom would this gift be directed? Against whose example could they measure this growth?*

- *Paul also prayed that the Thessalonians would have even stronger hearts (v. 13). What character qualities would this strengthening produce? These qualities would prepare them for what critically important future event?*

The cardinal virtue for Christians is always love. It is the central commitment of the two greatest commands (Mark 12:28–34). To desire and do what is best for the beloved is the essence of God's love for us. The missionaries had loved the Thessalonians like this, generously and self-sacrificially, as if they were their own family. Like a brother, a mother, and a father would, they showed the new believers how to love.

Now, Paul's wish for this new church was to experience lavish love from the Lord, but that was only a start. Once they were filled, Paul wanted God's love to fill them up to overflowing. He wanted love to run up to the brim and splash over toward one another within their fellowship. But that, too, was only the start. He wished that their love would continue to surge and swell until everyone else got a taste of this superabundant divine love of Christ.

Paul prayed that these young Christians would be spiritually prepared to meet the Lord. Since the Lord's return was closer every day, he prayed for their perseverance and maturity while they waited. He wanted their hearts to grow deep and strong in the Lord. He wanted their character to be transformed. He wanted them to be as holy as the other saints Jesus would bring back with him.

Paul's prayer in 3:11–13 was written in a formula that some scholars call a wish prayer. These prayers are sometimes used at the end of a letter as a final blessing before the farewell. However, as here, they may conclude a section before changing the subject. These prayers are most easily identified by opening phrases like *May the Lord...*or *I pray that you may...*followed by specific spiritual wishes for the readers. Churches have adapted some of these wish prayers for use in public worship as benedictions to conclude worship services.

- *This formula was common in first century writing, occurring in several New Testament letters. To see the variety of good wishes these prayers contained, look at those found in other letters. In the right column, list the blessings the apostles wanted for the recipients.*

| Recipient | Prayer | Wishes |
|---|---|---|
| **Church in Rome** | Romans 15:5–6 | |
| | Romans 15:13 | |

| | | |
|---|---|---|
| **Church in Corinth** | 2 Corinthians 13:14 | |
| **Church in Ephesus** | Ephesians 1:17–19 | |
| | Ephesians 3:16–19 | |
| **Church in Philippi** | Philippians 1:9–11 | |
| **Church in Colossae** | Colossians 1:9–12 | |
| **Timothy** | 2 Timothy 1:16–18 | |
| **Philemon** | Philemon 4–6 | |
| **Hebrew Christian Diaspora** | Hebrews 13:20–21 | |
| **Gaius** | 3 John 2–4 | |

## EXPERIENCE GOD'S HEART

- *Think of a time when your prayers were answered beyond your wildest dreams. How long did you have to pray before that answer came? How did you feel in the meantime while you waited for an answer? What kept you hopeful?*

- *Have you ever been isolated from Christian fellowship? What were the circumstances? Was it illness, travel, relocation, or apathy that kept you from fellowship? What convinced you to gather with the church again?*

## SHARE GOD'S HEART

- *Write a card or letter to a far-away believer you think of often. Maybe it is someone who influenced you to follow Jesus. Maybe it is someone you had the privilege to disciple. Tell them something about their walk with Christ that has encouraged you. Also, be sure to tell them how much you look forward to seeing them again face-to-face.*

- *Timothy's report was an enormous encouragement to Paul and Silas. Many pastors and missionaries must move on before seeing the results of their ministries. Does the previous pastor of your church know about the recent spiritual progress of people he cared for while he was there? Has the missionary who worked in your area heard about recent converts? Those are the things they live and work for. Call or email them and let them know.*

# Talking It Out

1. Obviously, a person in isolation can still follow Christ, but that should not be any Christian's normal experience. What aspects of the Christian life can you do alone? Which activities are difficult to do without gathering? Which ones are impossible to do without the company of fellow Christians?

2. Work together to write a wish prayer for your local church. Start with "May the Lord…" and finish with four or five specific spiritual blessings that you agree your church needs right now.

LESSON 6

# Loving and Living as Christians

(1 Thessalonians 4:1–12)

The American shad, a fish from the herring family, spends its entire life passing through hostile living conditions. Some begin life in the Schuylkill River of Pennsylvania, but they cannot stay there. As they grow, they must make their way to saltwater more than eighty miles away. Even there, the transitional environment of the Delaware Bay requires constant physical adjustments and adaptation to climate, temperature, and available food supply. Once at home in the Atlantic Ocean, the fish face hungry predators like striped sea bass and harbor seals.

Those that survive the sea make that harrowing transition in reverse, returning every year to the freshwater river where they hatched to spawn. This upstream journey results in the deaths of about sixty percent of migrating shad every year. In 1778, after that long ordeal, the fish arrived back in the Schuylkill River only to be devoured by George Washington's hungry troops at Valley Forge. Sometimes you just cannot catch a break.

For Christians, daily life can feel like surviving a hostile environment. Our society's worldview is our native environment, but new birth in Christ changes everything. From that point on, our schools and workplaces, social media, entertainment, and politics challenge Christian beliefs and moral convictions. Standing up to the onslaught demands constant vigilance and spiritual stamina. In the face of this constant barrage, many believers have given in to temptation's pressure or given up the struggle of faith altogether.

When Timothy returned to Paul and Silas with a relieving report about the Thessalonian Christians, he apparently brought some concerns as well. They were thriving in Jesus, but they still faced some difficult moral challenges, and they misunderstood some of what Paul had taught them. For the church to remain healthy, they needed some immediate encouragement and correction.

- *Besides teaching about the certainty of persecution, what else did Paul cover with them in their short time together (1 Thessalonians 4:1–2)?*

- *Primarily, was Paul encouraging them or correcting them? Whom did he say was the source of his ethical teaching?*

Try to imagine a sex-saturated society where sexual imagery is everywhere in art, commerce, and entertainment. Picture a culture where non-marital sex is rampant. Where multiple partners, sexual harassment, sex work, and child sexual trafficking are common. Where homosexual behavior, gender-bending, and public lewdness are normalized. Where ribald humor and shameless jesting are popular and predominant. Where it seems every moral boundary has been crossed. And where even some religious leaders applaud these perversions. In other words, try to imagine first-century Thessalonica.

Perhaps while you were reading this description, you thought to yourself, *I don't have to imagine a society like that; I am living in a society like that.* To be sure, as its adherence to Christian faith diminishes and the ethical restraints that go with it lose their hold, modern Western civilization looks increasingly like ancient Greece.

As the author of Ecclesiastes said, "There is nothing new under the sun" (1:9 NIV). Therefore, Paul's moral instruction to the Thessalonians is always applicable to others and directly so to Christians today.

- *What important area of Christian ethical behavior did Paul address first (vv. 3–5)? What was God's desire for them in this area? What fruit of the Spirit would help them in this area (Galatians 5:22–23)?*

- *Whose sexual ethics were these new Christians supposed to contrast with (1 Thessalonians 4:4–6)? Why might this have been difficult for the Thessalonians? Why was the new Christian sexual ethic so critical among believers in the church?*

- *List at least three of the five reasons Paul gave that their sexual behavior was expected to be different in Christ (4:3–8).*

Thessalonica was known for its licentious lifestyle. Extramarital sexual relationships were normal. Demosthenes, a popular Greek statesman, described the domestic sexual arrangements of the upper class: "Mistresses we keep for the sake of pleasure, concubines for the daily care of our persons, but wives to bear us legitimate children and to be faithful guardians of our households."[16]

From the moment of their new birth, persecution threatened the physical survival of the new Christians at Thessalonica. Since then, perversion threatened their spiritual survival as the holy people of God. They had to swim upstream in a libertine society surrounded by frescoes and statues, symbols and religious practices that were constantly appealing to sensual desires. Paul wrote bluntly to these believers that God had a different desire for them—sanctification.

## WORD WEALTH

The basic biblical meaning of *sanctify* is "to be set apart." Many qualities can separate us from the crowd, like outstanding athletic ability, physical deformity, or possessing the largest collection of baling wire. The biblical concept of sanctification includes such a separation, but the quality of our separation in Scripture is different. We, as God's children, are set apart *for a holy purpose.*

Many Roman Catholics will recognize the phrase *Sanctus, Sanctus, Sanctus* from the Latin Mass. It is usually inscribed on the tabernacle in which the communion wafers are kept. Then, just before the prayer to consecrate the bread, the congregation recites this phrase, a quote from the prophet Isaiah, "Holy, holy, holy is the Lord God, Commander of Angel Armies! The whole earth is filled with his glory!" (Isaiah 6:3). *Sanctus* means "holy." The root of the word survives in English words like *sanctuary, sanctity (of life), sanction,* and *sacrosanct.*

Through a variety of ceremonies, objects in the Old Testament temple were set apart for holy purposes. So were the priests and Levites. Offerings, too, went through a process to be made holy and fit for the purpose of worship. Paul told the Thessalonians that they were like these objects and people, being set apart from the rest of the world. They were on their way to holiness.

## The Way to Holiness

Because Jesus suffered on the cross for sin, those who have put their faith in Christ have, as far as God is concerned, had their sins absolved. When we respond with faith to the good news of Jesus, we are spiritually born again. This new life as a child of God has an immediate spiritual result: God declares us righteous. In this way, we are already holy.

However, any honest observer will note that we Christians are not always righteous in our behavior. We still sin. Often. In this way, we are not holy yet. Sanctification is the gradual process of our unholy behavior conforming to our new holy identity.

Upon new birth, God the Holy Spirit moves into the new believer's life. He begins to work in us to effect his change. Old sinful patterns that were comfortable start to feel unsatisfying. New spiritual habits that never interested us begin to look attractive. The indwelling Spirit convicts us of sin and affirms us in righteousness so that we move steadily, inexorably toward the holy character of Jesus himself. The more ingrained the old patterns are, the more obvious it is when God frees us from them. The more instinctive our old lifestyle was, the more miraculous when the Holy Spirit sanctifies us.

You may have heard people claim, "The Bible doesn't say that much about sex." Perhaps they haven't read it. More than half of the New Testament books offer some instruction about a believer's sexual behavior. In fact, taking the Bible as a whole can provide a robust and cohesive sexual ethic for our road to sanctification.

The New Testament teaches a sexual integrity that may seem foreign to us. Because we live in an era that disregards religious convictions, many Christians have grown up with very little scriptural teaching about sex.

- *While we do not have the space to craft a whole sexual ethic from the whole Bible, the following New Testament passages offer us some of the basic ideas. Write the Bible reference from the list below to the right of the corresponding principle.*

| Matthew 5:27–28; Matthew 19:1–9; Mark 10:6–9; Romans 1:21–28; 1 Corinthians 6:9–11; 1 Corinthians 6:16–20; 1 Corinthians 7:2–4; 1 Corinthians 7:8–9; Ephesians 5:22–33; Hebrews 13:4 | |
|---|---|
| *Sexual union is meant for one man and one woman until death.* | |
| *Marriage is God's provision for healthy sexual expression.* | |
| *Extramarital sex is a violation of the marriage union.* | |

| | |
|---|---|
| *Within marriage, sex can be holy.* | |
| *A husband's body belongs to his wife, and hers to him.* | |
| *Sexual unfaithfulness is a permissible reason for divorce.* | |
| *Sex is an important part of the self-giving love within marriage.* | |
| *Even our thoughts should be sexually pure.* | |
| *Some sexual behavior is a sign of rebellion against God.* | |
| *We can be forgiven and cleansed of our past sexual sins.* | |

## Sanctification and Sex

Because Thessalonian culture was so far from God's ideal sexual ethic, this was an area that required Paul's direct teaching. He urged the Thessalonian Christians to live a different life, one contrary to their old assumptions and instincts. They needed to learn self-control. Some of them needed to marry and be faithful to their sexual commitments within marriage.[17] Sanctification would require living contrary to their own culture, but they did not have to manage it on their own. The Holy Spirit would enable their holy life.

- *On the topic of sexual behavior, Paul repeatedly used the word holy. What do you know about being holy?*

- *What does holiness have to do with sex?*

- *Why do you think Paul concluded this portion of his letter by mentioning the Holy Spirit (1 Thessalonians 4:7–8)?*

For most modern readers, holiness is a foreign concept. Apart from some fusty, hyper-religious impressions, we don't really know what to think. Certainly, we wouldn't think of ourselves that way. Saints are holy, sacraments are holy, consecrated items or places are holy. But me? You must be joking!

That is completely the opposite of the biblical teaching about holiness. Every Christian, from the newest convert to the most mature leader, is called to holiness. Moses demanded it of the Jews (Leviticus 11:45–46), and Peter reiterated it for Christians: "Shape your lives to become like the Holy One who called you. For Scripture says: 'You are to be holy, because I am holy'" (1 Peter 1:15–16). If you are new to the biblical concept of holiness, the following resources may be helpful.

### *Video: Bible Project, "Holiness"*

This is a great place to start. The artists and teachers at Bible Project produced a quick summary of the sweep of the Bible's treatment of holiness, from God's perfect eternal character to our growing practical holiness (https://bibleproject.com/explore/video/holiness/).

### *Sermon: Alistair Begg, "Holiness: Hebrews 10:10–17"*

We cannot achieve holiness without the saving work of Jesus on our behalf. However, once we have come to God through him, holiness is the pursuit of every true follower of Christ (https://www.truthforlife.org/resources/sermon/holiness/).

### *Podcasts: Bible Project, "Holiness"*

In this three-part series of dialogues, Bible Project founders Tim Mackey and Jon Collins discuss the meaning and practical implications of holiness (https://bibleproject.com/podcast/series/holiness-series/).

### *Books*

*Pursuit of Holiness*, by Jerry Bridges (NavPress, 2016). Jerry Bridges was a lifelong leader and speaker with the Navigators, founded as a Christian discipleship mission to military servicemen. He wrote several books refuting the notion that spiritual growth just happens naturally to believers without any effort on our part. This book focuses on the practical steps we can take to grow in personal holiness.

*The Holiness of God*, by R. C. Sproul (Tyndale House, 2006). In this book, theologian and teacher R. C. Sproul explores the meaning of God's holiness. "We must seek to understand what the holy is. We dare not seek to avoid it. There can be no worship, no spiritual growth, no true obedience without it. It defines our goal as Christians" (13).

*Rediscovering Holiness*, by J. I. Packer (Crossway, 2021). Responding to the diminishing push for holy living in our culture, theologian J. I. Packer explains the lifelong role holiness plays in the Christian life. From the first steps of conversion to finishing well, a holy life is wholly dedicated to God.

### *Songs*

"Holy God, We Praise Thy Name," by Michael Card, from the album *Starkindler: A Celtic Conversation Across Time*, 2006. This fresh rendition of an eighteenth-century hymn notes first the holy character of God, then the holy transformation of his people, before turning to the angels' worship of his Holiness in heaven.

"Undone," Sovereign Grace Music, from the album *Sooner Count the Stars*, 2014. When we get a glimpse of the Lord's holiness, we are brought face-to-face with our own unholiness. In that encounter, we need his mercy and grace. Thankfully, the Lord generously offers both.

## Increase Your Love

Besides the moral dangers coming from outside the church, Timothy must have reported a serious issue growing within the church. As we will see, part of Paul's teaching in Thessalonians involved the victorious return of the Lord Jesus. It appears some of the new believers concluded that working a steady job was not a wise or heavenly use of the limited time they had left. In this first letter, however, Paul's primary focus turned to the subject and application of love.

- *What commendations did Paul give the Thessalonians about the way they loved one another (1 Thessalonians 4:9–10)? What exhortation did he give regarding love?*

- *What commonplace actions did Paul tell them would gain the respect of the non-believing community around them (vv. 11–12)? In what way would this mirror the example of Paul when he lived among them (review 2:8–9)?*

Since the specific timing of the Lord's return has never been our business, Paul urged these Christians to mind their own business and carry on with their work until Jesus does appear. And he commended them for their increasing love toward one another while urging them to live among unbelievers in ways that would command their respect.

## EXPERIENCE GOD'S HEART

- *How does living the Christian life feel like swimming upstream? Do you feel the pressure to conform to the pattern of this world (Romans 12:1–2)?*

- *What steps are you taking to be transformed by the renewing of your mind?*

- *Why do you think Scripture mentions sexual matters so often?*

- *How does controlling your body relate to the health of your soul?*

- *Who has taught you the most about the New Testament sexual ethic?*

- *Some doubt the power of the Holy Spirit to transform a life, but those who have been set free from past sin know what he is able to do. If you have experienced the sanctification of God's Spirit, especially in the area of sexual sin, talk to your church's youth minister. Offer to share your story of hope with the youth group.*

- *Set aside time for focused prayer for a Christian you know who is wrestling with sexual identity issues or toying with sexual sin. Write down a prayer for this person and return to it while you await progress.*

# Talking It Out

1. In the 1990s, a Christian men's movement called Promise Keepers encouraged men to join accountability groups to discuss issues of Christian character, including sexual integrity. Groups like this can prove helpful to both men and women. Consider asking a few of your friends to meet with you for personal accountability and prayer.[18]

2. Discussions of sexuality or sexual morality are often fraught with trauma. Sexual abuse, addiction, and shame keep many Christians from thinking deeply about sexual honor. So "like those who don't know God" (1 Thessalonians 4:5) in the world around us, sex becomes a topic of shame or shamelessness. When we recognize that there are personal issues that keep us from facing this topic, we should consider Christian counseling. A wise, trained counselor can help us navigate what blocks us from a life of sexual freedom. If cost is a factor, consider a local Bible college or Christian university, where students are seeking clinical experience in helping others overcome spiritual trauma.

LESSON 7

# Jesus Is Never Late

## (1 Thessalonians 4:13–5:11)

The canon's yeoman in Chaucer's *Canterbury Tales* utters the quotable phrase, "Better late than never." With it, he meant that when a thing needs doing, it is better to do it late than to never do it at all. We have been repeating this line ever since.

Usually, we use it when we are late for an appointment or slow in accomplishing a task. Better to arrive late than miss the date altogether. Better to miss the deadline than fail to perform at all. In every case, we are dealing with a time others have set in advance or that we have coordinated with others. To be late, we must be bound to their schedule.

An early scene in Peter Jackson's film *Fellowship of the Ring* introduces the relationship between Frodo the hobbit and the wizard Gandalf. We see Frodo reading peacefully beneath an ancient tree in a green wood. He hears the wizard humming while he drives his cart down the grassy lane. Frodo jumps to his feet with a smile and runs to confront Gandalf. Calling from the bank above the cart, "You're late!" he accuses.

The cart stops, and Gandalf the Grey slowly tilts his head so that his eyes can be seen from under the broad brim of his wizard's hat. "A wizard is never late, Frodo Baggins," he explains, "nor is he early. He arrives precisely when he means to."

Both friends have a laugh, and the point is clear: Gandalf is on his own schedule.

When others are on your schedule, you cannot be too late. A bride cannot be too late for the wedding. A corpse cannot be too late for the funeral. As Queen Clarisse in *The Princess Diaries* said, "A queen is never late. Everyone else is simply early."

Jesus cannot return too late. Generations of Christians have longed for his return to happen in their lifetimes, but for reasons only he knows, we continue to wait. It will happen on the Father's timeline, not a minute too soon and not a minute too late. We are on his schedule.

When Paul taught the Thessalonians about Jesus coming again, they must have been overjoyed. Their current circumstances of antagonistic neighbors and magistrates would come to an end. Their faith in Messiah Jesus would be vindicated. Others were bound to acknowledge their new King. All who waited faithfully for his coming would be rewarded for their devotion to him.

This confidence moved them to abandon their former religion. It buoyed them when persecution overwhelmed them. The whole community encouraged one another to believe no matter what. But then some of them died.

What would become of their dead loved ones? Would those who died miss out on Jesus' glorious return? Would they be included in the eternal kingdom? Would they reign with Christ like Paul had promised? Had Jesus come too late for them?

Timothy returned to Paul and Silas with questions like these from the new converts in Thessalonica. So Paul offered some additional clear teaching to calm their fears and kindle their hopes.

- *What analogy did Paul use to describe death (1 Thessalonians 4:13–15 and the study notes for these verses)?*

- *What is unique about the way that Christians grieve their dead? On what basis do we believe that our dead are not permanently lost to us (v. 14)?*

- *List the order of events Paul described at the second coming of Jesus (vv. 15–17). How will his return be unmistakably announced? Who will have the prominent roles in Jesus' vanguard? Where will the great reunion of all believers in Christ take place?*

- *What wonderful, endless promise do we have after that moment of his coming? How does knowing this shape our view of Christian death? What should be the effect of this promise on us (v. 18)?*

It wasn't too late for their dead loved ones. We will see them again. What a comfort! Life is full of goodbyes, but for Christians, there is always one more hello to look forward to. And, after that, no more goodbyes.

## THE EXTRA MILE

During Jesus' ministry, the most important Jewish leaders were from the religious party of the Sadducees. This faction believed and taught the Torah (the first five books of the Bible), but they rejected the traditions of the elders who interpreted it. They also rejected the immortality of the human soul because it was not taught in the Torah. Naturally, they denied eternal punishment and reward, heaven and hell, angels and demons, and the resurrection of the dead.

For Jews like them, death was the end. This life was your only life. Religious devotion, when it mattered at all, mattered here and now. Your satisfaction with it depended on the choices you made. Many people today feel the same way.

The Old and New Testaments teach differently, however. Both indicate the ongoing existence of the human soul, and the New Testament teaches it explicitly. Furthermore, throughout the Bible, there is a clear expectation that the grave is not the final resting place for anyone.

For a survey of Bible teaching about surviving death and ultimate resurrection, look up the following verses: Job 19:25–27; Psalm 22:29–31; Isaiah 25:6–8; 26:16–19; 66:22–24; Ezekiel 37:11–14; Daniel 12:2–3; Matthew 22:22–32; Luke 20:37; John 5:25–29; Acts 26:14–15; Romans 6:4–5; 1 Corinthians 6:14; 15:20–23; 2 Corinthians 5:1–10; Revelation 20:11–15.

If you have further interest in the Christian resurrection and heaven to come, check out the resources in the endnote.[19]

## Meeting the King

Paul assured the Thessalonians that at the resurrection, God had a plan for their beloved dead to be part of Jesus' return. In fact, they would have an honored role in that day of triumph. As Bible Project's Tim Mackie explains:

> Paul…uses language that would normally describe how a city subject to a Roman Caesar would send out a delegation to welcome or meet his arrival. Paul then applies this imagery to the arrival of King Jesus. He, too, will be greeted by a delegation of his people who will go to meet the Lord in the air as they welcome and escort him back to this world where he will establish his kingdom of justice and peace.[20]

As surely as Jesus himself rose from the dead, so would the Thessalonians' honored dead. Jesus' return will trigger their resurrection, and as they usher the King into his kingdom, the rest of us will join them in the air.

Christ's return will be no secret. We will not have to guess when it will happen. We will not have to deduce that it has. There will be no need to convince anyone to go here or there to experience it (Luke 17:22–24). It will be obvious. It will be witnessed everywhere. And it will come suddenly.

An angelic shout and the blast of a heavenly trumpet will announce the Great Reunion. Graves of the righteous from everywhere in the world will be emptied. Christians from everywhere, eager for his return, will rally to their long-awaited Savior. His triumph will be complete, and we all will be there to see it.

## DIGGING DEEPER

From the day Jesus ascended into heaven, his people have been looking forward to his descending back to earth. As generations anticipated his first coming at Bethlehem, new generations now anticipate his second coming. One Greek word for this "coming," "being present," "arrival," or "return" is *parousia*. One-third of its usage in the New Testament is here in Paul's letters to the Thessalonians.

The disciples asked Jesus, "Tell us…what sign should we expect to signal your coming [*parousia*] and the completion of this age?" (Matthew 24:3). He did not offer a date, but he was happy to describe the signs and effects of his coming.

- *Look up the following verses to learn some details about the coming of the Lord. If the verse describes a sign to expect, write it under Setting. If it describes the results of his coming, write it under Effects.*

| Scripture | Setting | Effects |
|---|---|---|
| *Matthew 24:26–27* | | |
| *Matthew 24:37–39* | | |
| *1 Corinthians 15:22–23* | | |
| *1 Thessalonians 3:13* | | |
| *James (Jacob) 5:7–9* | | |

| | | |
|---|---|---|
| *2 Peter 3:10–12* | | |
| *1 John 2:28–3:3* | | |

- *How did Paul view specific predictions about Jesus' return (1 Thessalonians 5:1–3)?*

- *How does Paul's view agree with Jesus' own teaching (Matthew 24:36; Acts 1:6–11)?*

- *What illustration did Jesus and Paul use to describe the surprise timing of the Lord's return (Matthew 24:42–44; 1 Thessalonians 5:2)?*

- *How is this image helpful? Why might it also be frustrating?*

- *What additional metaphor did Paul use to describe the certainty of Jesus' coming and its painful nature for many (1 Thessalonians 5:3)? Why will his coming be such a shock to non-believers?*

Though Jesus and Paul could not have been clearer, there has been no shortage of Christian predictions about Jesus' return. Church father Irenaeus (late second century) predicted that Jesus would return in the year 500. Baptist preacher William Miller (1782–1849) predicted Jesus' coming to occur on April 18 and then on October 22, 1844, launching the Adventist movement. German monk and mathematician Michael Stifel (1487–1567) calculated that October 19, 1533, was the date. In his 1970 book *The Late Great Planet Earth*, the late Hal Lindsey expected Jesus before 1988. NASA Engineer Edgar Whisenant wrote and distributed three hundred thousand copies of his booklet *88 Reasons Why the Rapture Will Be in 1988*, probably around September 12. We can cite hundreds of examples like this. Often, when someone makes a case for a new date and publishes it in a book, the hunger for a specific prediction leads to millions of sales.

Even the disciples wanted to know. They asked Jesus for the details on at least three occasions (Matthew 17:10–13; Mark 13:3–4; Acts 1:6–7). In every case, Jesus batted the question away. Rather than answer their direct question, he gave them a string of predictions and a description of what the state of the world would be when he returned.

Essentially, he told them that the date of his return was none of their business. Instead, they should get on with the business of taking the gospel to all the people groups on earth (Matthew 24:14). Every day that he waits is another opportunity for new people to experience his salvation (2 Peter 3:9).

Paul gave the Thessalonians the same instructions. He told them not to worry about dates or times. That is God's business. Jesus will come, unannounced, like a thief at night, and those who are not awake and waiting for him will be devastated.

- *If a specific date is not to be known, how will Jesus' return be unsurprising to believers (1 Thessalonians 5:4–7)? Why should we not be startled or unsettled that he will one day return? What three metaphors did Paul use to contrast those who have trusted in Christ and those who have not?*

- *While we wait for his return, what posture should we take (vv. 8–9)? What preparation should we make to fight the battle until he comes? What armor should we use?*

- *To close this portion, Paul returned to the assurance he gave in 4:17–18. What was that promise (5:10–11)? And what can we do with it?*

As certain as labor after a pregnancy, as certain as the pains of labor, the Lord will come to rule and judge the world. The rest of the world will be startled, even terrified, by his coming, but believers in Jesus will not be startled that he returns. They may not know when, but they know he will. They are not worried about his judgment because they are safe from his righteous wrath. They have trusted in Jesus and his atoning death for their sins, so they can wait confidently for his return.

Until he returns, there will be struggles. Persecution and opposition will be normal. Hatred and rejection will be commonplace. Influencers will try to stop us from preaching and believing the good news. They will discourage and harass believers wherever we go. So we must take the battle seriously with level-headedness. To engage in this spiritual battle, we put on the armor that God offers for the fight (Ephesians 6:10–18). We put it on daily, standing steadfastly until that great day of victory when the battle is finally over.

The return of Jesus is nothing for Christians to dread. In fact, it is a source of great delight and encouragement. His promises of restoration and peace will be fulfilled. His people will join him in victory. Our dead will be raised. Our struggle with sin will be over. Our enemies will be ashamed. Our Great Reunion will begin and never end.

The good news of Jesus includes this good news. It fills his people with courage and hope as they wait eagerly and sometimes impatiently for his return. It keeps us working, growing, and worshiping until then.

## EXPERIENCE GOD'S HEART

- *Have you been to a Christian funeral lately? Was it for someone close to you? What was it like?*

- *How does confidence about the return of Jesus fill you with hope at the graveside of someone you loved? Why is Christian grieving different?*

- *How much have you thought about or studied biblical prophecy? Some churches specialize in it. Others barely speak of it. How does what you have learned up to now square with Paul's teaching and what you have read here?*

## SHARE GOD'S HEART

- *Not everyone will be overjoyed by Jesus' coming. Some will be ashamed of their lifelong lack of response to Jesus. Pray that the hard-hearted people you know will respond to God's grace before he returns.*

- *The return of Christ gives our mission a sense of urgency, but whether he comes in our lifetime or centuries from now, he remains present with us and in us through his Holy Spirit. This is not the case with unbelievers who live without this reality and hope. Be attentive for opportunities to talk with others about the good news, including the second coming of Jesus. When you see someone who needs this news, speak up.*

# Talking It Out

1. Discuss with your small group how knowing a specific date for Jesus' return would affect you. If it were soon, what would change? If you knew it was still a long way off, what would change? What is the wisdom of not knowing when the last day will come?

2. Talk about how you feel about Christ's return. If it happens soon, are you excited? Does it fill you with dread? Are you worried? Will you be relieved? Did you doubt it would happen? Will you be disappointed to miss out on potential milestones you had set for yourself?

LESSON 8

# Practicing the Presence

(1 Thessalonians 5:12–28)

The last suitcases are in the car. The freshman college student looks awkwardly at her parents standing together on the front steps of her childhood home. What do you say when you face those last moments together before the next life adventure begins? So much history. So much love. What can be said?

With the big things already said and the next step imminent, what comes naturally is a string of instructions. Simple, healthy advice before the goodbye.

- *"Did you pack your phone charger?"*
- *"Don't forget to change the oil in your car before you come home at Christmas."*
- *"Say hi to Marty and Sarah for us when you see them."*
- *"Here's some cash for the road."*
- *"Study hard and have some fun."*
- *"Pull over and rest if you get tired."*
- *"Let us know when you get there."*
- *"Phone your mom every weekend."*
- *"We love you, kiddo."*

In most of Paul's letters, this is the pattern. After teaching the core doctrines and addressing the important issues in the church, he often closes with a string of brisk instructions. Sometimes they are practical: *Prepare a room for me. Collect my manuscripts and bring them with you. Greet the friends who live there.* Sometimes they have more spiritual content: *Watch out for divisive people. Stand firm in the faith. Be wise in your dealings with non-believers. Pray for us.*

Both letters to the Thessalonians follow this pattern but especially the first. Paul already encouraged the believers in their progress. He reminded them to expect persecution for following Jesus. He explained his concern about their perseverance. He recounted the relieving report that Timothy brought. He exhorted them toward sexual integrity in tempting circumstances. And he corrected some of their confusion about Jesus' return. Having already covered the topics that required many words, he turned to the topics that required few.

## Loving One Another

- *To which members of their community were they supposed to show recognition (1 Thessalonians 5:12–13)? What three things were these people doing for the health of the church? How would peaceable relationships between the believers help them carry on their work?*

- *Take note of the action verbs in verses 13–15. What were the Thessalonians commanded to do and for whom?*

- *What instruction would the derelict Christians need (v. 14)? Why did Paul single out the insecure as those who needed encouragement? How could they help the weak in faith? How does patience relate to all this interpersonal advice?*

- *Compare Jesus' Golden Rule, "In everything you do, be careful to treat others in the same way you'd want them to treat you" (Matthew 7:12), with Paul's command (v. 15) regarding how to treat one another inside and outside the Christian community. How is Jesus' teaching more sweeping? How is Paul's more specific?*

During Paul's and Barnabas' first missionary journey in the Galatian region, the apostles passed twice through each community. On the first pass, they preached the gospel to establish a believing community. Then they retraced their steps and appointed leaders in each Galatian town (Acts 14:23). Not much time had passed between visits, but it was enough for the missionaries to recognize which of the new Christians had maturity and skill.

In Thessalonica, this did not happen. Because the missionaries' presence in their city was cut short and the magistrates seemed to have forbidden their return, the young church was left to make leadership decisions on their own. So here Paul gave them pointers for how to single out the right people, not merely to give them encouragement but also to assign them spiritual authority.

> The policy of Paul and his colleagues seems to have been to wait until qualities of spiritual leadership displayed themselves in certain members of a church and then urge the others to acknowledge and respect those leaders. One of the most obvious qualities of leadership was a readiness to serve the church and care for its needs. Such leaders did not do the appropriate work because they had been appointed as leaders; they were recognized as leaders because they were seen to be doing the work.[21]

Recognizing leaders, however, did not preclude the other believers from ministering to one another. The unruly, the insecure, the weak, and the offenders needed special attention from others. These are the very ones it might have been easier to ignore or sideline in the community. They required more energy and great patience to include. Paul knew this, and he insisted that the other believers make an effort for the ones who were needier.

## Loving the Lord (Together)

After laying out the Christian's social obligations, Paul turned to habits of non-stop Christian living. Like breathing and the heartbeat, these practices needed to become the spontaneous, continual, life-giving practices of the Thessalonian believers.

- *What three snappy commands did Paul give the believers (1 Thessalonians 5:16–18)? How frequently were they to do these things?*

- *What attitudes do these three continual practices produce in the Christian?*

- *How would those attitudes help a believer no matter the situation? Can you see why God would want this non-stop Christian living for them?*

"Continual," "always," "in the midst of everything." These words tell us how often to rejoice, pray, and give thanks. If this seems impossible or even impractical, perhaps we can learn from a humble French monk named Lawrence.

Nicolas Herman grew up a poor peasant in seventeenth-century France. He enlisted in the military during the Thirty Years War, in which he was injured and was further crippled fighting in other skirmishes as a civilian. He attempted domestic service but, due to his disabilities, proved inept and awkward in this role. From his fighting days onward, he was drawn more and more deeply into religion, so in June 1640 he joined a monastery in Paris. Nicolas remained there the rest of his life, taking the religious name Lawrence of the Resurrection.

Brother Lawrence was not well-educated nor well-connected, and his physical limitations kept him from striking an impressive posture. These factors led his supervisors to assign him the most menial tasks in the community. Lawrence embraced this humble role and used the tedious, repetitive tasks to learn discipline and devotion. He found he could pray while washing the cups, meditate while sweeping the floor, and sing while repairing the sandals of other monks. His simple, steady service and genuine, deep love of God attracted others who sought him out for spiritual direction.

Some of his brief letters of advice and recorded conversations became the devotional classic *The Practice of the Presence of God.* His direction sounds like a soul that has taken Paul's instructions in 1 Thessalonians 5:16–18 to heart. For example, he advised:

> We might accustom ourselves to a continual conversation with Him, a conversation free of mystery and of the utmost simplicity. We need only to know God intimately present in us, to address ourselves to Him at every moment, to ask His aid, to discern His will in doubtful things, and to do well those things we see clearly He is demanding of us, offering

> them to Him before doing them and giving Him thanks for having done them for Him after we have done them. In this continual conversation we are likewise unceasingly engaged in praising, adoring and loving God for his goodness and perfection.

And:

> Our sanctification depends not upon changing our works but in doing for God what we ordinarily do for ourselves. The best way of reaching God is by doing ordinary tasks, which we are obliged to perform, entirely for the love of God. It is a great delusion to think that time set aside for prayer should be different from other times, that we are equally obliged to be united to God by work in the time assigned to work as by prayer during prayer time. Prayer is simply an awareness of the presence of God.[22]

Before we move on, let us consider another way to understand these three short commands in 1 Thessalonians 5:16–18. Because the previous paragraph and the one to follow are about their life together in Jesus, some scholars see these three commands as descriptions for the church when it gathers.[23] Rather than a perpetual rejoicing, praying, and thanking for the individual, the church gatherings are always joy-filled, prayerful, and grateful. Whenever the church meets, they should always be doing these things.

Whether Paul directed his instructions to the whole church or to the individual, these non-stop Christian practices are what God wants for his people (v. 18).

## Loving God's Word

- *How could the Thessalonians have stifled the spiritual vitality of their churches (5:19–22)? To what natural force does Paul compare the Holy Spirit?*

- *What attitude toward prophetic teaching were the Thessalonians supposed to have? Were they to trust all prophecies? What steps did the Christians need to take with prophetic teaching?*

In the days before the New Testament was completed, Christians studied the Old Testament together. Paul and the other apostles could preach the good news of Messiah Jesus and defend faith in him from the Law and the Prophets (the two major divisions of the Hebrew Scriptures). Additionally, the early Christians heard regularly from prophets. These Christian men and women did not have the same authority as the apostles, but they did claim to deliver messages from the Lord. The apostle Peter encouraged everyone with a speaking ministry to speak as though God were speaking through them (1 Peter 4:11).

Many preachers and teachers today have the same confidence. Their study of Scripture has led them to their beliefs and convictions under the guidance of the Holy Spirit. With this confidence, they can stand before the gathered church and declare, "Thus saith the Lord!"

Paul wanted the Thessalonians to take new prophetic messages seriously but not unquestioningly. He did not want them to pour cold water on prophets or turn up their noses at these words. But, as every Christian knows, many claim to speak for God who do not. Paul's solution, then and now, was to test the prophetic preaching. Receive all prophecy respectfully but sift it all carefully. Keep the good and discard the bad.

## DIGGING DEEPER

Paul told the Thessalonians to test every prophecy, but he did not explain how. There must have been a standard for evaluating whether the preaching was square with God's heart. Indeed, there was.

Recall that when Paul and his friends were driven from Thessalonica, they went to the town of Berea. In Acts 17:11, we read that "the Jews of Berea were of more noble character and much more open minded than those of Thessalonica. They were hungry to learn and eagerly received the word. Every day they opened the scrolls of Scripture to search and examine them, to verify that what Paul taught them was true." In other words, they applied a test even to the words of the apostle. Whatever Paul taught had to be in keeping with the previously revealed written Word of God. The Bereans were not uncritically accepting any new teaching without investigation. Still other passages in the Bible provide us with a variety of tests for sorting the good from the bad.

Even today, we need not reject prophetic preaching, but we must always test it.

- *Below is a list of biblical tests that can be applied to the teaching of anyone claiming to proclaim God's Word. Look up the passage on the right and fill in the blanks in the statements on the left explaining each test. The first one is done for you.*

| **Tests for Weighing Prophetic Messages** | |
|---|---|
| The teaching must be in keeping with the _Scriptures__. | *Acts 17:11* |
| The preaching will affirm the divine and ____________ natures of Jesus. | *1 John 4:1–3; 2 John 7–10* |
| There will be good _____________ from the ministry of a true prophet. | *Matthew 7:15–20* |
| The message must emphasize the _______ of Christ, not human effort. | *Galatians 1:6–9* |
| Believers with the spiritual gift of ________________ should weigh in on the teaching. | *1 Corinthians 12:10* |
| The message will _________, _________, and _____________ Christians. | *1 Corinthians 14:3–4* |
| Other prophetic teachers should ___________ the message. | *1 Corinthians 14:29–32* |
| The preaching should lead to ____________. | *1 Corinthians 14:33* |

## Final Wish Prayer

In saying goodbye, Paul closed his letter with another wish prayer, the expression of hope for their continued progress toward holiness. In some ways, this benediction expressed his longing for every individual in the Thessalonian Christian community and for the community itself. Oh, that this longing would be fulfilled in us too!

- *How did Paul describe God's character in his closing wish prayers for them (1 Thessalonians 5:23–24)?*

- *What desire for them did he repeat from earlier in the letter (4:3)? Does the second wish prayer here contrast, deepen, or complete the first (5:23–24)?*

- *What ministry could these new Christians perform for Paul and friends (5:25–27)? What sign of affection was customary for those within the church? Who was supposed to hear the words of this letter?*

# EXPERIENCE GOD'S HEART

- *Do you see your own personality in the list of those singled out for extra attention (5:14)? What kind of impact would it make on you if you received the care Paul called for?*

- *Do you know someone on this list? How would giving them that attention help them grow?*

- *How are you doing with continual joy, perpetual prayer, and ceaseless gratitude?*

- *What helps you with non-stop Christian living?*

- *What is keeping you from it?*

## SHARE GOD'S HEART

- *Pray for someone you know who is disheartened or feeling inadequate. Pray for them to be strengthened and filled with courage. Buy them a coffee and follow Paul's instructions. Encourage them.*

- *When will you worship again with your church? Think about how much better your shared life in Jesus will be if you arrive with a joyful, prayerful, grateful spirit. In the days between now and then, ask God every day to help you cultivate that spirit. Then join in worship with your whole sanctified self.*

# Talking It Out

1. Think together as a group about the people in your church who labor among you, who offer pastoral care and sound teaching in the Lord. They may or may not be in positions of official leadership. Does the congregation acknowledge or appreciate them? Designate a member of your group to write an appreciation card to the people you agree fulfill this role and have everyone in the group sign it.

2. Discuss how you feel about people, apart from the biblical authors themselves, teaching with the confidence that their message is from the Lord. If any in your group are from charismatic church backgrounds, they may even have experience with teachers who are called prophets. What are some dangers of extra-biblical prophets? What might be some benefits of a present-day ministry like that?

LESSON 9

# What's Coming to You

(2 Thessalonians 1:1–12)

Have you ever eavesdropped on someone's phone call? You are trying to mind your own business, but they are just a little *too* loud when they answer a call in the café. The issues are obviously important to them because their voice rises in pitch and volume. Their emotional tone seems more personal than business-like. The long pauses between their input make you curious about what the person on the other end of the line is saying. Someone needs their help and advice, but things are not going well. The call abruptly ends, and the talker rushes out, leaving you curious and a little embarrassed that you got caught up in someone else's affairs.

Paul's letters to the Thessalonian Christians are like that one-sided call. His first letter was written in response to the report Timothy brought back to Paul about the well-being of the new Christians. We didn't hear the report. We can only piece together its content from Paul's response to it. We learn about the issues they were struggling with by the issues he addressed in his letter. We are left wondering about the specifics, but we can surmise the big ideas.

Written and delivered, Paul's first letter did its work. The church was encouraged, rebuked, and instructed. Still, the Thessalonians had more questions for Paul and misunderstandings that needed answers. We don't have any copies of that correspondence from the Thessalonians. Maybe it was delivered verbally by the same messenger who carried Paul's first letter. Because we only have one side of the conversation, we don't know exactly what they asked or reported.

Like the first letter, we can piece together the Thessalonians' half of the conversation by carefully reading Paul's reply. The first letter addressed some important issues, but it didn't settle them. In fact, Paul needed to revisit each of the three biggest concerns, as the second letter indicates.

So Paul wrote a follow-up letter less than a year after he sent the first one.[24] In it, he assured his young Christian friends that their persecution would ultimately be resolved, that God's timing for Jesus' return is perfect, and that Christians must keep busy until his return, honoring God in their everyday lives.

Apparently, the second progress report he received about them was just as good as the first. After his initial greeting, he acknowledged their encouraging spiritual growth.

- *What two Christian virtues were still increasing in the Thessalonian church despite their continued difficulties (2 Thessalonians 1:3–4)? What was the nature of the difficulties they faced?*

- *What do you think it means that these virtues were growing in them? How would an observer like Paul know that faith and love were increasing in them?*

The persecution of the Thessalonian Christians continued relentlessly. And the "reward" for following Jesus was more suffering. Again, we don't know the specifics of this. Was Jason's household targeted again? Had they been fined, imprisoned, beaten, or worse? Were they scattering to nearby cities like the Christians in Jerusalem had done when persecution broke out there (Acts 8:1, 4)? Maybe all these things were happening. We just don't know with any certainty.

What we do know is that these Christians needed the assurance that God's justice would be done. Justice is getting what one deserves. They needed to know that following Jesus wasn't all tears, that the reward for faith was more than pain. They needed to know that their oppressors would not ultimately skate without consequences. They needed to hear that God noticed the treatment they were receiving from their enemies, *his* enemies, and that he would set things straight.

- *What did the persecution the Thessalonians were enduring and their spiritual growth in the midst of it indicate about God's appraisal of them (2 Thessalonians 1:5)? How was persecution a sign of their acceptance by God?*

- *Why may they have needed a reminder of the Lord's ultimate justice (vv. 6–7)? What will happen to their troublers? What will God do for the troubled? When will this justice be obvious to everyone? Describe Jesus and his entourage on that day.*

- *Who will face the Lord's punishment on that day (vv. 8–10)? What sentence will they receive?*

- *Who will have nothing to fear on that dreadful day? Instead of retribution, what will these blessed souls receive from the Lord? How will their triumph be linked to his?*

- *Why did Paul say the Thessalonian Christians were included in this glorious destiny?*

The Lord will set things straight. The tormentors will face torment themselves unless they repent. They will not get away with their mistreatment of God's people. Having heard and rejected the saving gospel, they will miss out on the chance to know the Lord and his forgiveness. The day of the Lord holds nothing but dread for them.

On the other hand, those who have believed the good news will be included in his glorious future. They will welcome his return. They will relish his victory. He will lift them up from their sorrow and humiliation to an eternal position of joy and prominence. He will delight in them, and they will delight in him forever.

The essence of glory is a tremendous weight or significance. It is often pictured by brilliant light (Exodus 34:33–35; Luke 2:9; Matthew 17:2). To glimpse God's glory is to see his weightiness, his ultimate significance, his magnificence. It is to marvel at the brightness of his character, his nature, himself. On that day, when Jesus the Just returns in blazing glory with all his holy ones to judge the world, his holy people will glorify him.

If you've ever been to a stage play, you know that the main character is often set apart from the others. How do they do that? With a spotlight. The director tells the crew to shine a powerful special light on the person the audience must notice. You can overlook everyone else, but you must pay attention to this actor.

When we glorify God, we are doing something like that. We are not only acknowledging that he is worthy of that kind of notice, but we are also shining the light on him so that others will see him too. Our worship, our living, our witness, our passions, our priorities can shine the light on Jesus. In doing so, we communicate to each other and the world about his significance, his magnificence, his importance. That's how we glow with his glory. That's how we glorify him.

Paul prayed this for the Thessalonians. He assured them that they would positively glow with the glory of God when everyone else would miss out on it. But they didn't have to wait until then. They could glorify him in the meanwhile. Their character could draw attention to Jesus' character. The good fruit of their faith could show the productive, healthy, and abundant life Jesus promised. The worthy lives they lived would show the world how worthy Jesus is. He would glow in them, and they would glow in him.

While we wait for that glory, we must continue in the confidence that the Lord will set things straight. Eventually.

Meanwhile, Christians like the Thessalonians endure the long days between the promise and the keeping. They suffer physical abuse in confinement, beatings, torture, and death. They suffer socially through jeering, ostracization, isolation, and neglect. They suffer financially under confiscations, vandalism, unemployment, and homelessness. They suffer, day after long day. The wait for justice can seem interminable.

The troubles that Christians in first-century Greece faced still plague the world today. Indeed, worldwide persecution is on the uptick. In 2023, more than 365 million Christians worldwide (one in seven) faced high levels of persecution for their faith, many of them suffering terrible violence. Nearly 5,000 were murdered, over 4,000 were arrested, and 14,766 churches and Christian-run schools, hospitals, and cemeteries were attacked.[25] In Canada alone, more than one hundred churches have been vandalized or destroyed by arson since 2021.[26]

When will these evils be punished? When will God's people be vindicated?

## DIGGING DEEPER

This question has been on the lips of believers since Old Testament times. When we look at the world from inside our troubles, our perspective is limited. We cannot grasp the timescale of God or his longsuffering patience with rebels.

As we learned in Lesson 7, he has postponed Christ's return because of his mercy. Every day that passes provides opportunities for new souls, even persecutors, to hear, to respond to, and to believe the good news. Second Peter 3:9 tells us that any seeming delay in his return "reveals his loving patience toward you, because he does not want any to perish but all to come to repentance."

However, time for persecutors and repentance will run out. The last martyr will die for Christ. The last Christian will be arrested and imprisoned. The final beating for the sake of Christ will take place. The last believing teen will be shunned by her family. The unjust will face God's justice. The merciless will long for mercy. And God's own people will be swept up into his glory.

When will all this happen? God only knows. *How long, O Lord?*

- *Look up the Bible passages listed in the lefthand column, and then in the middle and righthand column, provide your answers to the questions concerning who is longing for justice and the nature of their suffering.*

| Scripture | Who is longing for justice? | What is the nature of their suffering? |
|---|---|---|
| *Psalm 13* | | |
| *Psalm 35:11–17* | | |
| *Psalm 74:4–12* | | |
| *Psalm 119:84–88* | | |
| *Habakkuk 1:2–4* | | |
| *Zechariah 1:12–13* | | |
| *Revelation 6:9–11* | | |

- *Did you identify with any of the sufferers in the preceding Bible passages? Did you feel their pain, their longing for God to put things right? If you did, what about their pain and longing did you relate to?*

We do not know when the return of Jesus will be, but when it happens, no one will miss it. The Lord Jesus will be revealed from heaven in a blaze of glory and accompanied by an army of angels. He will return as a conqueror to subdue all his enemies and carry out justice.

What a contrast this is with Jesus' first coming! His incarnation, though the most profound miracle of history, happened quietly. He came as a human embryo, slipping into the world almost unnoticed, announced in secret to a young, unmarried virgin. Born in a stable, nestled in a manger, and wrapped in rags, he started life humbly enough. His family fled from a local despot to an undisclosed location in a foreign country. They returned to a village in rural northern Israel, a place so obscure that even the disciples scoffed at its unimportance (John 1:46). Jesus slept outdoors, ministered among peasants, and surrounded himself with the uneducated, unrespectable, and unclean. Truly, Isaiah the prophet correctly predicted the nature of his first coming:

> He sprouted up like a tender plant before
> the Lord,
> like a root in parched soil.
> He possessed no distinguishing beauty
> or outward splendor to catch our
> attention—
> nothing special in his appearance to make
> us desire him.
> He was despised and rejected by men,
> a man of deep sorrows
> who was no stranger to suffering and grief.
> We hid our faces from him in disgust
> and considered him a nobody, not worthy
> of respect. (Isaiah 53:2–3)

His second coming will be no such understated arrival. Announced by a blaring ruckus-piercing trumpet and the unignorable shout of his chief angel (1 Thessalonians 4:16), he will arrive. He will appear in the sky so that everywhere every eye will see him

(Matthew 24:27; Revelation 1:7). His own Jewish people, most of whom refused to acknowledge his first visit, will mourn over the way they rejected and treated him (Zechariah 12:10–14). Those who believe in him he will gather to him in the sky for all the world to witness (1 Thessalonians 4:17). And then, every human soul, those who gladly accepted him in this life as well as those who stubbornly refused to, will bow before him and acknowledge that he is their rightful Lord and Judge.

Until then, the door to salvation is open. Every humble, repentant soul who comes to Jesus now will look forward to the incomparable glory of his second coming.

We don't have to wait, however, for him to be glorified in our lives. An obedient child of God is a credit to his Father. A sinner saved is a credit to the Savior. Sanctified Christians, full of spiritual fruitfulness, are a credit to God and his steady, patient work in our lives. He shines when we shine, so that is what Paul prayed for the Thessalonian Christians.

- *What two specific things did Paul regularly pray for the church at Thessalonica (2 Thessalonians 1:11–12)?*

- *What would happen if those prayers were answered?*

Paul explained to them in his first letter that God wanted them all to be sanctified (1 Thessalonians 4:3), to be set apart for holy purposes. God's desire for every Christian is to live a righteous life that imitates his holy character. A sanctified life like that would be suited for the kingdom of God.

The bad news for every sinner is that we cannot become fit for the kingdom of God through our efforts (Romans 3:20–26). We cannot hone our character, alter our habits, or purge our sins enough to achieve spiritual worthiness. We all sin and fall short of the glory of God. The good news, however, is that we do not become worthy *in order to be* saved. God pronounces us worthy *because* we are saved.

Only Jesus, through his sin-free life, sin-atoning death, and sin-conquering resurrection, was a human worthy of God's kingdom. His works on our behalf satisfied God's righteous standard. His righteousness is the free gift of God's grace for anyone who believes. That is how we become worthy of God's kingdom.

Paul's prayer for the Thessalonians was that the gap between their living and their calling would be constantly narrowed. He wanted their thoughts, attitudes, and behaviors to conform completely to the worthiness granted to them through Jesus. On their first day of faith, they were spiritually ready for eternity. But God desired even more for them—for every spiritual son and daughter to become like his Son in every way achievable. And that is what daily sanctification is all about.

Furthermore, Paul prayed that the Lord would grant them success in the courageous spiritual exploits they set out to do. These were not the Big Hairy Audacious Goals bandied about in corporate strategy seminars, not a sort of Dream Big, Do Big motivational talk. Paul expected that their growing faith in Christ would lead them to want good, God-oriented things and would lead them to do specific spiritual work.

For example, when Paul wanted to return to Asia minor (Acts 16:1–3), he wanted to do the Holy Spirit's good will, and his faith prompted him to cross over into Europe instead. The fulfillment of that desire and faith-prompted work was the salvation of his Thessalonian brothers and sisters. They were the results of his faith-inspired ministry. Paul prayed that they would experience the same kind of sanctified and fruitful life in Christ that he was living.

## EXPERIENCE GOD'S HEART

- *A missionary asked an African Christian to name his favorite Scripture passage. In response, this brother, who had endured serious, life-threatening persecution, quoted all of Psalm 3, including, "Strike all my enemies on the jaw; break the teeth of the wicked" (v. 7 NIV). How do you feel about this desire for God to punish our oppressors? Is there a place for imprecation in our prayers? How does this desire fit with the New Testament principle in Romans 12:19?*

- *The state of the whole world can break your heart. Maybe the headlines make you nervous. Maybe they make you angry. Often, they just make you sad. Isn't it a relief to know that the Lord has a plan to make everything right? If you know it, pray the Lord's prayer (Matthew 6:9–13), and linger on the request, "Manifest your kingdom realm, and cause your every purpose to be fulfilled on earth, just as it is in heaven." Think about the situations that are not in line with his will. Pray that things will change, but pray it now with the confidence that one day they certainly will.*

# SHARE GOD'S HEART

- *Jesus told his disciples to pray for those who mistreat them (Luke 6:28). Often these are family members, coworkers, fellow students, or various kinds of officials. Pray for someone who is antagonistic toward you and your faith.*

- *Some of the works inspired by our faith will place us in danger of verbal or physical attack. Sharing the gospel in some settings, for example, can draw hostility. Standing up for the innocent can incur risk. Have you ever been prompted by God's Spirit to speak or act in a way that would put you in jeopardy? Did you do it anyway? What were the results?*

# Talking It Out

1. Tell each other one or two reasons why you are looking forward to the day of the Lord.

2. Strangely, the longing for the second coming is missing in many modern churches. It is easy to see why a suffering, persecuted community of Christians might eagerly long for Jesus' return. Discuss together what factors might keep Christians from that yearning. Is there enough teaching on it in the church? Are Christian lives too comfortable and risk free? Is it healthy *not* to look forward to the arrival of God's justice?

LESSON 10

# You Can't Miss It

## (2 Thessalonians 2:1–12)

"Jesus already returned. The prophecies about Jesus coming back were fulfilled when Jerusalem was destroyed by Titus in AD 70."

The sincere Christian sat across the table and explained how he had come to that conclusion after reflecting on Matthew 16:28, "I promise you, there are some standing here now who won't experience death until they have witnessed the coming of the Son of Man in the presence and the power of the kingdom realm of God!" He then began to research an end-times belief called "full preterism" (PREH-tur-izm) or fulfilled eschatology and insisted that Jesus had already returned.[27] Eschatology is that part of Christian theology that deals with end-times matters, such as the rise and rule of the Antichrist, the rapture, the resurrection of believers and unbelievers, the second coming of Christ and his reign, the final judgment, and the new heavens and the new earth.[28]

A person might be shocked to hear someone say that the second coming is history rather than an event still to come. You may be surprised that such a belief even exists. Looking at the world that is and comparing it to the world described after the triumphant return of Jesus, is it possible that we missed it? Is it possible that the whole world missed it? Could we miss the second coming of Christ?

That was a central question of both Paul's letters to the

Thessalonians. In 1 Thessalonians, the young, persecuted Christians were asking about the second coming of Christ. They believed that Jesus would return soon, just like Paul had taught them. Jesus would come and deliver them out of their troubles and into the new kingdom ruled by Jesus the King. But they wondered if he was coming too late. Some of the Christians there had already died, perhaps by persecution. The believers had already taken their lifeless bodies and buried them in the earth. If Jesus returned now, wouldn't these dead Christians miss out on his glorious return?

We know the answer to that concern. Paul's answer was to point them to the familiar return of a conqueror to his home territory. As he approached the city, an official escort would go out to meet him on the outskirts. Then the victor would enter the city with all his faithful supporters at his side. Paul assured these Christians that their beloved ones who had already died would have the tremendous honor of accompanying King Jesus as his faithful supporters, his official entourage, at his triumphant return (1 Thessalonians 4:13–18). They wouldn't miss it. And no matter when *you* die, you cannot miss it either.

Somewhere between these two letters to the Thessalonians, another angle on this same problem became an issue. If Jesus didn't come too late, maybe he came too soon. Maybe he had already returned when we weren't looking, and we didn't notice. Maybe we missed his glorious return.

They wouldn't have been asking this question in the way that we might today. *Did Jesus come in a secret rapture and leave us behind?* The idea of a rapture didn't fully develop until the 1800s. Rather, the Thessalonians would have wondered whether Jesus had returned and if he was ruling somewhere imperceptibly, and the current state of the world was just how things were going to be from now on. More like the preterist view.

Is this just how things are in the kingdom? Is this the fulfillment Jesus promised? Has he already returned? Did we miss it?

- *Where did this strange idea come from that Jesus had already returned (2 Thessalonians 2:1–2)?*

- *What three effects was Paul afraid this false teaching had on the Thessalonian Christians (vv. 2–3)?*

Don't be confused. Don't be disturbed. Don't be deceived. Paul said the Thessalonians should not let this false teaching shake them from the teaching they had already received. They needed to tighten their grip on what the missionaries had taught them. They needed to remain calm and unflappable even in the face of this disturbing idea. They had to avoid falling for the trick, for the doctrinal error.

These doubts had been planted by people claiming that Paul himself taught this. So Paul spelled it out for the Thessalonians. They would not miss Jesus' coming. In fact, they would be unable to miss it. Furthermore, he assured them, it had not happened yet because it could not have happened yet. Other events had to occur first.

- *What is the title of the human figure who must appear prior to the second coming of the Lord Jesus (vv. 3–4)? What political or military campaign will he lead? What posture will he take toward God?*

- *What blasphemous steps will he take? Where will he do this great evil?*

- *Is this the first time that Paul has mentioned this character to them (vv. 5–7)? What was restraining this person from bursting onto the scene?*

Paul assured the Thessalonians that before Jesus would return, the outlaw must lead the rebellion. Who is this outlaw, this man of lawlessness? Wouldn't we love to know? There have been many candidates for that role. Emperors Nero and Diocletian,

Pope Innocent III and other popes, Mao, Hitler, and other dictators, several US presidents, UN secretaries-general, and so on. The sad fact is that a world in rebellion against God produces a steady string of serious contenders for this ultimate leader of immorality and evil.

We do not know who he is. Paul did not spell it out. Perhaps this is because he was clear about it when he taught the Thessalonians in person, so he saw no need to repeat it in his letter. Perhaps he was purposely vague because we are expected to leave this category open to ongoing historic auditions for this role. One of these great and terrible men will be *the* great and terrible man. We just don't know when he will appear or who precisely he will be.

However, we are not completely in the dark. We do know what he will be like. He will be the supreme outlaw or the lawless one. Some Bible translations call him "the man of sin."

In one sense, all of us are men and women of sin. We are rebels who live contrary to God's law. We sin. We like to sin. We are condemned because of sin. Our sin earns us death. Our sin leads us away from Christ the only Savior, but because of his grace and mercy, God the Son came looking for us. He took on our sin and paid our penalty, and he saves his people from their sin.

By contrast, this man will be so identified with rebellion, so lawless, so sinful, that this is what will define him. He will refuse to be bound by any rules, any laws, any virtue, any moral restraints. The man of sin will be lawless, and he will receive the full consequences for his sin.

- *What is his destiny? Who will easily defeat him? When will he be destroyed (v. 8)?*

- *Describe the methods he will use to deceive people (vv. 9–12). What spiritual power will back him?*

- *Which people will be misled by him? What response to the gospel makes them susceptible to his deception?*

- *What role will God play in this end-times happening (v. 11)?*

Paul introduced the outlaw with his complete story arc, like writing his obituary on the day of his birth. The conclusion of the story is already written. He is already condemned. He is destined for destruction. He will not win. In fact, he will be no match at all for King Jesus. The breath of his mouth, the glory of his arrival, will blow this would-be rival away forever.

The outlaw will oppose God. This is why so many have been falsely labeled the Antichrist. It is because they were *anti*-Christ. Ruthlessness, scorn, hostility, pressure, and villainy perpetrated against believers have been constant since Peter and John were bludgeoned for preaching the gospel. The frequency of this abuse is increasing, and the pressure is intensifying. In the past century, more Christians have been martyred by more atheist *anti*-Christs than in all of history combined.

This future lawless man will dwarf them all in his anti-Christ posture, but meanwhile, there will be other antichrists. John the apostle predicted a slew of them:

> Dear children, the end of this age is near! You have heard that Antichrist is arising, and in fact, many enemies of Christ have already appeared, and this is how we know that we are living in the closing hour of this age. For even though they were once a part of us, they withdrew from us because they were never really of our number. For if they had truly belonged to us they would have continued with us. By leaving our community of believers they made it obvious that they never really belonged to us.
>
> But the Holy One has anointed you and you all know the truth. So I'm writing to you not because you don't know the truth, but because you do know it, and no lie belongs to the truth.
>
> Who is the real liar but the one who denies that Jesus is the Christ. He is the real antichrist, the one who denies the Father and the Son. (1 John 2:18–22)

## DIGGING DEEPER

In three years of public ministry, Jesus explained the signs of his second coming to the disciples only (Matthew 24; Mark 13; Luke 21). The rest of the time, when he taught about his return, he used parables. Parables were an indirect way to teach through metaphor and analogy. Parables pointed to the truth while provoking the imagination so that his hearers could mull over his meaning with further thought and prayer.

- *Read the following three parables. (It helps to read them aloud.) After you have read them, think about the characters in the stories. Do any of the characters represent Jesus? Do any of them represent his followers? Do any of them represent his enemies? How do the characters respond to Jesus' return? Then try to sum up the main lesson of the parable in a single command or short statement.*

| Parable | Passage | Metaphors | Main Lesson | Other Thoughts |
|---|---|---|---|---|
| *Serving an Absent Master* | Luke 12:42–48 | | | |
| *Unprepared to Wait* | Matthew 25:1–13 | | | |
| *Giving Account* | Luke 19:12–27 | | | |

## Realities to Come

The outlaw, the God-opposer, will also be blasphemous. He will be like Lucifer himself in Isaiah 14 or the satanic king of Tyre in Ezekiel 28, who exalted himself above God, seeking to usurp his throne and rob him of his glory. This future man will be devilish in his ways.

And just as his master is a counterfeit, he will be a counterfeit too. He will do things the way that Satan does, parading as a powerful, admirable angel of light (2 Corinthians 11:14). He will do miracles and powerful tricks that deceive the world.

Jesus' gospel did not put us in spiritual danger; we were already in danger. His first coming did not put us in jeopardy of judgment; we were already condemned. Jesus came to save. He came to provide a way out. He came to show us the way to the Father. He came to deal with our sin. He is the means of mercy. We must trust him to know God.

The people who will be sucked in by the outlaw's deceit are those who have already refused to receive Jesus' good news by faith. Like he did with the pharaoh of the exodus, the Lord hardens the hard. He deludes the deluded. He judges those who reject his mercy. This will be the fate of the outlaw and his followers.

Paul mentions a "prevailing" or restraining power that must be taken away for these things to unfold (2 Thessalonians 2:7; see also TPT note 'c' for this verse). The Thessalonians knew what it or he was, but Paul didn't spell that out here. Was Paul referring to a government or leader? Some Christian teachers see the rapture of the saints in this verse, suggesting that the removal of Christians from the world will unleash this rebel. Others say it is the restraining power of the Holy Spirit. We don't know what or who the restrainer is, only that he was restraining the lawless one from arising then and still is today.

One day, however, this restrainer will go. The Satan-empowered rebel will rise. The rebellion will start. Only then will the second coming happen. Neither the Thessalonians nor we have missed it or will miss it.

Paul was principally concerned that his believing friends should not be alarmed. In fact, those who love the truth and are saved do not need to be afraid of the deception of the wicked deceiver or the wrath of the righteous judge.

Jesus told his disciples, "What I say to…you, I say to everyone—be awake at all times!'" (Mark 13:37). We need to be attentive and ready for his return. These events will unfold. Maybe we will be the generation that gets to see it all. Maybe we will recognize the supreme outlaw, maybe not. But we will certainly *not* miss Jesus' return.

While we wait for his arrival, we can trust him no matter what antichrist is troubling us at the minute. No matter how much sin and rebellion and blasphemy and counterfeiting we see, Jesus, the returning conqueror, will blow it all away. Easily.

## EXPERIENCE GOD'S HEART

- *What Christian teaching have you heard about Jesus' return? Would you say you have a lot or a little knowledge of what the Bible has to say about it?*

- *List a handful of other passages you know that talk about that future hope. Then read one to see the similarities it might have with 2 Thessalonians 1–2.*

- *Does thinking about the antichrist, the last rebellion, and the end of the world fill you with hope or dread? Does it confuse or disturb you? Why? Can you see how trusting Jesus protects us from overwhelming anxiety about it?*

## SHARE GOD'S HEART

- *Many Hollywood films are about a post-apocalyptic world because there's a huge market for it. Probably many of the people you know are curious about it. Start an interesting conversation. Ask them, "Have you ever thought about the end of the world?" If they respond, the content of Paul's letters to the Thessalonians should come in handy.*

- *Two large international cults send workers door-to-door. Among their frequent conversation starters are questions about Jesus' return. Have you ever engaged them about this? Are you afraid to? What would give you the confidence you need to have the discussion?*

# Talking It Out

1. Tell the others in your group what you noticed in the parables of Jesus' return from this chapter's Digging Deeper exercise. If the message wasn't clear to you, ask the others for their input. Talk about how the knowledge that Jesus may come at any minute influences the way you live.

2. Read together 2 Thessalonians 1:5–10 and 2:10–12. Compare God's justice toward persecutors to his justice toward all unbelievers. Now read what Jesus said about everyone who does not believe in him, John 3:14–18. Talk about why unbelief is punishable. End by praying for the hard-hearted in your family or your local community.

LESSON 11

# Shoulder to Shoulder

(2 Thessalonians 2:13–3:5)

Besides the expected spring snowmelt, a steady rain had fallen for days. The river was rising slowly but relentlessly, and the experienced townspeople got busy. Some went down to the water's edge to defend the town. They hurriedly stacked sandbags in a long wall of protection against the swelling torrent. Others put their backs into shoveling sand from the sandpile into empty sacks about sixty feet from the river. From there, a line of townspeople, young and old, relayed those bags to the workers on the frontline.

This hard labor continued for hours while the waters rose and the wall of sandbags grew. Fresh workers periodically replaced the weary ones who needed a break. At the church fellowship hall nearby, volunteers prepared nourishing meals, filled water jugs for the workers, and entertained their young children in the gym.

All these efforts paid off. The flood did some damage, as expected, but the worst was avoided. Homes and businesses were spared. The relieved town had much to celebrate.

Who saved the town? The sandwich makers or the sandbag stackers? The human chain delivering sandbags to the edge or the truck driver delivering the sand to the site? The pastor rallying his church members or the mayor rallying his city employees? The first shift of volunteers or the last ones?

The answer, of course, is that all of them saved the town. They all tackled the challenge together. They all participated in the mission.

## Together

As Paul prepared to close his letter, he reminded the Thessalonians that they were all in Christ together. He prayed for them; they prayed for him. They faced opposition; he faced opposition. They stood for the gospel; he stood for the gospel. They all participated in the life of Christ; they all participated in his mission. They all played a part.

- *Make a note of five ways Paul contrasted the Thessalonian believers with those who would be deceived by the man of lawlessness (2 Thessalonians 2:10–14).*

- *Why would this prompt Paul to give thanks for the Thessalonian believers?*

- *How would these qualities give the new Christians confidence?*

After describing the antichrist rebel and the children of his rebellion, Paul turned his attention back to the children of God. They were an altogether different type of people. Their response to the good news of Jesus proved that they were the Lord's handpicked people. Others may resist or reject the Lord's message and messengers, but God's children receive it with joy. So they had the love and calling of God, his Spirit was making them holy, and they had his glory to look forward to.

## WORD WEALTH

Ancient Greek script was written in uppercase letters without spaces or punctuation. That was saved on papyrus, but sometimes it leads to confusion for translators. For example, translations differ on the proper understanding of 2 Thessalonians 2:13. The translation depends on where to place spaces in the text. If the phrase in question contains two words (*ap archz*), it would mean "from the beginning," as The Passion Translation has it. This would indicate that God's choosing of these believers took place at the start of his redemption plan. But if the phrase contains only one word (*aparchz*), it would mean "firstfruits," indicating that these Christians were the first part of the larger crop of believers to come.

While The Passion Translation reads "by choosing you from the beginning," it also gives a nod to the "firstfruits [in the harvest] for salvation" in the footnotes. The confusion is understandable because both alternatives are true. God's choosing of the Thessalonians was from the beginning *and,* as we learned from 1 Thessalonians 1:6–8 where the gospel rang out from them, they were the first believers of many more to come.

## Do This

- *What did Paul expect the Thessalonians to do with their special status in the Lord (2 Thessalonians 2:15)? What spiritual asset did they have to help them do this?*

All these benefits of life in Christ were the basis of Paul's next command. These strengths would be necessary for the hard work that lay ahead of them. The mission they had joined when they trusted Jesus was ongoing. The persecution they had experienced to this point was not going to stop. The opposition would be fierce. So they must not quaver, waver, or abandon their posts.

With the wonderful status they had with the Lord, they could be strong. Furthermore, with the excellent authoritative teaching they received from the missionary team, they could be confident.

The precise word used for these teachings was *tradition.* Paul passed on to them teaching that he himself had received from a Spirit-filled authority (1 Corinthians 11:2). This sequence of inherited teaching was to be a source of confidence to them. It didn't originate with them or even with Paul but ultimately with the Lord and his first apostles.

Some theologians today maintain that this passage implies that church traditions can be just as (or nearly as) authoritative as Scripture. They believe that practices and interpretations that are passed down through the church must be followed. But that is more than this passage teaches.

In fact, most mentions of tradition in the New Testament are derogatory (Matthew 15:1–6; Mark 7:1–13; Galatians 1:14; Colossians 2:8). Jesus often ran into the obstinate obstacle of tradition. Opponents of his ministry appealed to traditions handed down to them from human religious authorities to disapprove of his way of doing things. Tradition wasn't and isn't necessarily a good thing. It can be stifling. And the traditions used against Paul certainly were.[29] In response, Jesus made a clear distinction between God's authority and that of the religious leaders. We need to maintain that distinction today.

This is how theologian and Bible commentator John Stott explains Paul's use of tradition here:

> These [traditions] are not the later traditions of the church, but the original teachings or traditions of the apostles. It is vital to preserve this distinction between the two kinds of tradition. The apostolic traditions are the foundation of Christian faith and life, while subsequent ecclesiastical traditions are the superstructure which the church has erected on it. The primary traditions, to which we should hold fast, are those which the apostles received from Christ,...which they taught the early church by word or letter, and which are now preserved in the New Testament.[30]

It is this tradition of the apostles that Paul taught the Thessalonians in word when he was with them and by letter when he taught them from afar. With the confidence of their position in Christ and their confidence in this message of Christ, they had the resources they needed to stand fast.

- *In your church, list some teachings that you are sure come from Scripture.*

- *Now list some instructions that you are confident come from tradition.*

- *Are the teachings of tradition treated as equally authoritative and binding as the biblical teachings are? Or does your church do a fairly clear job of distinguishing between tradition and biblical teaching, giving greater deference to biblical doctrine than to church traditions? Explain your answer.*

## Shoulder to Shoulder in Prayer

Thinking about the task ahead and the challenges the Thessalonian Christians would face, Paul was moved to pray.

- *Where would they get the power to stand firm and keep the faith (2 Thessalonians 2:15–17)? How is God described in this wish-prayer?*

- *What effort did Paul ask them to pray about (3:1)? How did he want the gospel to go forward and be received?*

- *How did Paul want them to pray for his personal safety (3:2)? Who was troubling him?*

- *How did this prayer request for himself prompt him to encourage the Thessalonians again (vv. 3–4)?*

Paul's prayer for their strength and encouragement led him to ask for mutual prayer. This time, the request is more specific than in his first letter (1 Thessalonians 5:25). The Thessalonians weren't the only ones facing challenges. Paul and his friends continued to encounter opposition to their message. They needed the church to stand with them in prayer.

In Corinth, Paul faced an incident similar to the one that drove him from Thessalonica (Acts 18:12–17). Jews conspired, formed a mob, and dragged him before the Roman authority. In this case, all the accusations were religious in nature, so the proconsul dismissed them, but the atmosphere remained charged with the non-believers.

The missionaries needed their Thessalonian brothers and sisters to remember these dangers and pray. First, Paul wanted the good news to spread quickly (literally "to sprint forward") and be as readily received and believed as it had been with them. Second, he wanted protection from the wicked, faithless enemies.

## DIGGING DEEPER

It is Sunday morning, the singing has concluded, and you open your Bible in preparation for the pastor's sermon. Instead, he approaches the pulpit to introduce a guest speaker. A missionary who is usually stationed overseas is back in North America visiting churches, giving updates on their mission's progress, and raising support.

"Oh brother," you mutter under your breath, "another financial appeal."

Missionaries have made appeals since the beginning. They have always depended on their partnerships with the rest of the church. Like the workers stacking sandbags at the water's edge, they depend on countless others to provide the means to carry out their ministries. We are in the worldwide gospel mission together, whatever our specific role.

Missionaries have always needed partners to pray for them. They need individuals and churches to provide financially for their efforts. They need practical help, too, like technology and communication assistance or food, lodging, and transportation when they are visiting. Without that support team, the missionary would be severely limited in his labors.

## Help Wanted

Even the first generation of apostles needed assistance. They needed colleagues like Paul had in Barnabas, Mark, Luke, Silas, and Timothy. But beyond that, they also hoped that the new Christian communities would engage with their missions and support them as they spread the gospel wherever they went.

- *Read the following Scripture passages. Notice the specific appeal that the Lord's worker makes. If it is for prayer, jot down the request. If it is for meeting a practical need, indicate that too. Finally, consider your involvement with missions. If it is something you have done to partner with a missionary, check the box ☑ on the far right side. As you do this exercise, think of missionaries you know of and consider what partnerships they may need. Pass the sandbag. Let's do this together.*

| Passages | Partnership Opportunities | ☑ |
| --- | --- | --- |
| *Matthew 10:40–42* | | ☐ |
| *Luke 10:5–8* | | ☐ |
| *Acts 16:14–15* | | ☐ |
| *Romans 15:23–24* | | ☐ |
| *Romans 15:30–32* | | ☐ |
| *1 Corinthians 9:4–14* | | ☐ |
| *1 Corinthians 16:5–6* | | ☐ |
| *2 Corinthians 11:8–9* | | ☐ |
| *Ephesians 6:18–20* | | ☐ |
| *Philippians 4:10–19* | | ☐ |

| | | |
|---|---|---|
| *Colossians 4:2–4* | | ☐ |
| *Philemon 1:22* | | ☐ |
| *3 John 1:5–8* | | ☐ |

Paul's reference to the faithless put him in mind of the Faithful One. Both the apostles and the newer disciples could depend on the Lord through all their trials.

- *What final two qualities did Paul pray they would experience (2 Thessalonians 3:5)? Based on this portion of our study, why might they need this prayer to be answered?*

The apostle Paul was inspired to pray again for the Thessalonian believers to experience deeper love and steadfastness. These prayers of Paul for this Christian community revealed his understanding of the mutual relationship we have because of Christ.

These were not only converts; they were also partners. These were not only his disciples; they were also his brothers and sisters. They faced the same kinds of trials because they were on the same mission, grounded in the same gospel. Most importantly, they had the same faithful Lord to lead them into his love and into the future.

## EXPERIENCE GOD'S HEART

- *How do you see your role in the mission of the church? Are you a frontline worker like an evangelist? Do you play a support role in spreading the gospel? Do you see yourself as a partner to others in Christ's call to the nations?*

- *You could learn a lot about someone if you could read their prayer diary. You would see there how much they prioritize world evangelism. How often do you pray for the Lord's work around the world? Do you pray for specific people groups?*[31] *Do you intercede for any specific missionaries? Indicate below what and whom you pray for in terms of mission.*

## SHARE GOD'S HEART

- *Think about the way Paul described Christians in 2 Thessalonians 2:13–14. Does knowing these things are true about Christians give you confidence to share your faith with others? If you are loved, chosen, saved, called, and sharing in Christ's glory, what holds you back?*

- *To learn courage and dependence on the Lord, volunteer for a month with a local mission or evangelism effort. Explain to the director that you want some experience spreading God's Word. Join in as a learner and absorb as much training as they offer. Then go and participate in what God is doing nearby. You will grow as you go.*

# Talking It Out

1. Discuss with your small group how confidence in the Bible's authority helps you walk with Christ. Tell one another why you are persuaded the Bible's message is true and why it matters that the apostles got their message from Jesus himself.

2. Adopt a missionary. Often the church secretary posts the latest prayer bulletin from a supported missionary, where it languishes until it is replaced by the next one. Your small group can choose one of these ministries to adopt. Read their letters. Learn the names of their family. Email them to tell them of your interest. Ask them about the particular challenges they face where they are. See if there has been encouraging progress or disappointing setbacks. Your small group might even take up a collection or commit to monthly support for their ministry. And by all means, pray for them!

# LESSON 12

# Keep Busy

## (2 Thessalonians 3:6–18)

As we have seen, Paul's letters to the Thessalonians reveal a preoccupation with the return of Christ. This was not purely theoretical or theological interest in eschatology (the study of end times). It also had affected the way they grieved their dead, suffered under severe persecution, and managed their daily lives.

A preoccupation with the return of Christ can lead to strange conclusions. In the 1970s, one family, convinced that Jesus' return was imminent, gave away bags of clothes and shoes. They had purchased them big enough for their children to grow into, but with the Lord about to return, they wanted someone to use them immediately. So the recipients wore those clothes…out. The children whose clothes were given away grew up and reared their own children, who are now too big for those clothes.

Throughout history, people who don't think there will be a tomorrow tend to live like that. Why reform public education or prisons or health services if the Lord is returning to set everything straight any day now? Why work hard to buy a house, advance in your career, or save for retirement if none of those things are likely to happen before Jesus comes back?

This seemed to be the case in Thessalonica. In this second letter to them, Paul already mentioned two groups disturbing his friends in the church. In chapter 1, he wrote about the persecutors. In chapter 2, he warned about false teachers unsettling them about the return of Jesus. In the final chapter, he turned to a third group of troublemakers, the idlers.

- *How did Paul describe these problem Christians (2 Thessalonians 3:6)?*

- *From whose work ethic were they all supposed to learn (vv. 7–9)?*

- *What economic support had the missionaries received from the Thessalonians? Because of this policy, what did the missionaries have to do instead?*

- *What was the motivation of the missionaries for making these sacrifices?*

- *What principle did Paul teach the Thessalonians about work when he was with them (v. 10)? Why do you think he took such a hard line?*

- *Where do you think Paul heard the reports about these "unruly" Christians (vv. 11–13)? What kind of "busy" were they?*

- *What did Paul demand that these lazy believers do? What does he expect of the others?*

## WORD WEALTH

Some of the Thessalonian Christians were "unruly" or idle. The original word has colors of both ideas in it. It speaks of disorder, a life not ordered, out of order, like a soldier who marches out of step or quits marching with his regiment altogether. It speaks of those who stopped working and were living unproductive and disruptive lives.

The footnote in The Passion Translation is helpful here. It notes that the word *unruly* means "'undisciplined' or 'lazy' or 'not in battle order' or 'not in your duty station.' There is an implication that there were believers who refused to work for a living. Paul is implying that the church should not financially support those who refuse to work. Personal responsibility is a common theme in Paul's teachings."[32]

## Avoid Idleness—Work

Idleness is disruptive. With too much time on one's hands, there is time for personal sin, of course, but there is also time to stir trouble in the rest of the church and community. The old saying goes, "Idle hands are the devil's workshop." An old saying, indeed. Medieval poet Chaucer quoted it in his *Canterbury Tales*, and Paul agreed.

Now Paul believed he had a right to financial help. This has always been God's way. A legitimate religious leader could count on the financial support of those who benefited from his ministry. From the Old Testament priests right up through the modern evangelist, these religious workers were not required to go without.

Paul could have insisted on the Thessalonians' support, but he wanted to show them how to work hard. So he did ministry, *and* he worked a job as a tentmaker. He worked long hours for their sakes. To show them how to work hard, he refused to accept any of their resources. His example taught them how to wait for Jesus to return.

Just in case they didn't learn from his model behavior, he instituted a practical rule: No work, no food. Idleness will not feed you. Hunger is the best motivator to get busy. This rule helped the individual remain productive until the Lord's return. It also kept the rest of the Christian community from being burdened with disruptive, unproductive idlers.

- *Have you ever gone hungry? What led you to that situation? How did you handle it?*

- *Are you prone to avoid work? If so, why? If not, why?*

It is every able person's responsibility to feed themselves. This seems strict and maybe harsh in the modern welfare states of Europe and North America. It is especially difficult to square with in the post-COVID era, when we look back on a billion people who were sent home to receive government stipends *not* to work. But our first defense against hunger is our own two hands. If we want food in the fridge or soup on the table, we must earn the money to pay for it.

Our modern social welfare systems often short-circuit this principle. It would be easy to whistle past this idea, but when the Bible speaks to something, we should address it, even when it involves a controversial political or economic theory. The Bible has a practical and comprehensive social safety net. It goes something like this. We work to eat (Proverbs 10:4; 12:27; 19:15; 20:13).[33] We do not take the earnings of another person's work to feed ourselves. We do not presume that their resources belong to us. Even the poor were expected to work (Exodus 23:11; Leviticus 23:22). Paul made that clear here in 2 Thessalonians 3:10 and in 1 Thessalonians 4:11 (see also Ephesians 4:28). He did not simply urge believers to live like this; he *ordered* them to do this with the authority of the Lord Jesus.

We must acknowledge that some people are physically unable to work because of age, disability, or illness, so there must be an economic safety net. Again, the Bible is clear. When a person cannot provide for themselves due to health, injury, age, or disability, their family should step in. Paul writes in 1 Timothy 5:8, "If a believer fails to provide for their own relatives when they are in need, they have compromised their convictions of faith and need to be corrected, for they are living worse than the unbelievers." Even unbelievers recognize the responsibility to care for their own kin. Maybe they have burned their bridges with family. A crisis of physical need is a reminder to maintain or mend those relationships.

Some people who cannot work do not have kin either. Again, the Bible is clear. Neighbors should help out (Leviticus 25:35; Deuteronomy 15:7). Moses told Israel to "love your neighbor as yourself" (Leviticus 19:18 NIV). Jesus said the same but expanded it to include anyone whose unmet need we see and can meet, like the Good Samaritan did.

Some people can't work, don't have kin, and don't have neighbors who can help them. Then the church is the safety net. If the poor are in the family of God, this is obvious. From the start of the church, "the apostles gave powerful testimonies about the resurrection of the Lord Jesus, and great measures of grace rested upon them all. Some who owned houses or land sold them and brought the proceeds before the apostles to distribute to those without. Not a single person among them was needy" (Acts 4:33–35).

Another New Testament description of this principle can be found in 2 Corinthians 8–9. There we're told that the whole region was suffering, work dried up, and the family and neighbors of the needy were just as desperate due to the severe famine in Judea (Acts 11:27–30). When Christians elsewhere heard about the physical needs of their brothers and sisters in Christ, they took up a collection and delivered this money. Out of love, the generous voluntary contributions of believers for believers were a powerful symbol of Christian oneness and love. In the biblical safety net, the church is not the first support, but it must be there when other supports fail.

Each of these layers is natural and personal. They flow from already-established supportive relationships. We know our family. We know our neighbors. We know our brothers and sisters in Christ. Better still, we usually love them. Their plight matters to us, and so does their recovery.

Each of these layers also has accountability in it. Since we know them, we know when we are being taken advantage of. We know if they are truly in need or simply too lazy to feed themselves. We know if they have fallen into hard times or if they are perpetually making poor decisions. A little genuine hunger can motivate the lazy and mature the irresponsible.

If there is a role for the unnatural, impersonal, unaccountable support of governors and kings, it should be after these other layers fail.

> *If you are prone to idleness, do not imagine that others are obliged to provide for you. Paul commands you in the Lord Jesus to get to work. Do something useful for others. Take a job, any honest work, to serve your needs, the needs of others, and most importantly, the Lord. As Colossians 3:23–24 says, "Put your heart and soul into every activity you do, as though you are doing it for the Lord himself and not merely for others. For we know that we will receive a reward, an inheritance from the Lord, as we serve the Lord Yahweh, the Anointed One!"*

# DIGGING DEEPER

Provision is not the only reason that we work and perhaps not even the primary reason. We work because through our productive engagement with the world and other individuals, we cooperate with God. In his original creation mandate, our Creator invited human beings to participate with him in ruling the earth and its resources (Genesis 1:28; 2:15, 19–20). When we do this well, we fulfill our potential as his image-bearing partners in the world.

- *Below are a variety of passages that give a biblical overview of the purpose and value of work. On the left is the principle taught there. Match the passage to the principle. Check the endnote for the answers.*[34]

| **Principle** | **Related Scripture** |
|---|---|
| A. *Besides his ministry, Jesus did ordinary work.* | A. Genesis 1:26–28 |
| B. *Our work must not be our reason to live.* | B. Genesis 2:15 |
| C. *Godly work will continue in heaven.* | C. Genesis 3:17–19 |
| D. *The Lord is our true supervisor at work.* | D. Exodus 20:8–11 |
| E. *God assigned people to manage his creation.* | E. Deuteronomy 8:17–18 |
| F. *We need a routine rest from our work.* | F. Psalm 90:17 |

| | |
|---|---|
| *G. Christians depend on the Lord's blessing to prosper.* | G. Proverbs 14:23 |
| *H. Human sin caused work to be a hardship.* | H. Ecclesiastes 2:17–23 |
| *I. People were originally made with work in mind.* | I. Mark 6:2–3 |
| *J. Our ability to earn money comes from God.* | J. Colossians 3:17 |
| *K. Hard work is the way to wealth.* | K. Colossians 3:23–24 |
| *L. Any work should be oriented toward God's glory.* | L. Revelation 22:3 |

## Avoid Idle People

- *What if someone didn't conform to Paul's instructions about work? What were the compliant believers to do (2 Thessalonians 3:6, 14–15)? How did Paul expect this action to affect the idle Christians? What was Paul's hope for the restoration of their fellowship?*

- *How would this teaching apply to churches today?*

It is appropriate to avoid people who will not work. They will disrupt your life. They will drain your resources. They will waste their lives. They will misrepresent the gospel. And if you're not careful, you will help them do it.

So don't be drawn into the disorder of their idleness. Don't let their marching out of step with Paul's teaching cause you to stumble. Speak to them about it. Warn them about it. And if there is no remorse or change, back away. Paul teaches us to let them live with the consequences of their idleness.

We should take this difficult step from a place of love. We are not backing off because of anger, exasperation, or vengeance. We are not giving up on them or burning the bridge of a future relationship. We continue to think of them as a brother or sister in the faith (Matthew 18:15; Galatians 6:1). We remain hopeful that they will come around. In fact, restoration is the goal, but its achievement is not inevitable.

## Signing Off

- *With what blessings did Paul start and end his letter (1:2; 3:17–18)?*

- *What was the primary desire Paul expressed in his final prayer for the Thessalonian Christians (3:16–18)?*

- *Why do you think his appeal to peace was important as he wrapped up his letter?*

## While We Wait

Jesus is coming again! Both letters to the Thessalonians revolve around this great truth. Christ's return holds out hope for the suffering church and motivation toward holiness while we wait. His perfectly timed second coming will place an end date on hardship and a start date on glory. The expectation of the Master's return keeps us busy and productive so we can provide for ourselves and be generous toward others. Until that glorious day, we carry on trusting him and living faithfully while we wait.

## EXPERIENCE GOD'S HEART

- *Not all the people you know can work or find work right now. Based on the Bible's teaching about work and generously providing for those in need, do you have any responsibility to others? What has the Lord enabled and prompted you to do?*

- *How do you think about your own work? Is it a productive way to feed yourself and your family? Does it produce enough extra to be generous toward others and the Lord? Do you think of it as a calling? How does work motivate you to follow Jesus? How does a steady, honest job testify to the character of Christ?*

## SHARE GOD'S HEART

- *Does your church have a benevolence fund, a budgeted amount to contribute to the poor in your community? Most churches do, and most have policies for whom they will help. Learn about this aspect of your church's ministry. Ask your leaders how they distribute these funds and what stipulations are placed on the giving.*

- *Pray for those in your life who are seeking employment. The situation can be depressing, demoralizing, and depriving. Pray that the right door will open soon for an ennobling, productive position. Pray that they will have the courage to take that opening when it comes. Ask God for an opportunity to encourage them. And, when you can, help them find work opportunities that will meet their needs.*

# Talking It Out

1. Discuss how idle living leads to meddlesome habits. What happens to someone with too much time on his hands? What ill effects do the people in the families experience because of their idleness? What ill effects do the people in their church experience?

2. Paul's solution requires a warning and then withdrawal of fellowship from a busybody. These steps require a Christian community to be united in addressing the problem. Discuss the difficulty of doing this in a modern Christian church. Why might the idler not respond well? Why might church members be unwilling to follow Paul's teaching? How might the busybody avoid the lesson?

# Endnotes

1. Brian Simmons et al., "A Note to Readers," *The Passion Translation: The New Testament with Psalms, Proverbs, and Song of Songs* (Savage, MN: BroadStreet Publishing Group, 2020), ix.

2 For more information about synagogues in the ancient world, see W. White Jr., "Synagogue," in *The Zondervan Pictorial Encyclopedia of the Bible*, 5 vols., edited by Merrill C. Tenney (Grand Rapids, MI: Zondervan, 1976), vol. 5, 554–68; E. Yamauchi, "Synagogue," in *Dictionary of Jesus and the Gospels*, edited by Joel B. Green and Scot McKnight (Downers Grove, IL: InterVarsity Press, 1992), 781–84; and B. Chilton, "Synagogue," in *Dictionary of the Later New Testament and Its Developments*, edited by Ralph P. Martin and Peter H. Davids (Downers Grove, IL: InterVarsity Press, 1997), 1141–46.

3 M. N. Tod, "Thessalonica," Bible Study Tools, accessed June 13, 2024, https://www.biblestudytools.com/encyclopedias/isbe/thessalonica.html; Philip W. Comfort, "The Social and Geographical World of Thessalonica," in *Lexham Geographic Commentary on Acts through Revelation*, edited by Barry J. Beitzel (Bellingham, WA: Lexham Press, 2019), chap. 44.

4 John B. Polhill, *Acts*, vol. 26 in The New American Commentary series (Nashville, TN: Broadman Press, 1992), 361n57.

5 In Greek, Acts 17:6 uses the title *politarchs* for these Thessalonian officials. Bible critics once claimed this was an example of an error in the Bible's texts because this title is not used in other Greek literature. However, Luke was too careful a researcher (Luke 1:1–4; Acts 1:1–2) to make up this term. Archaeology at the city's Vardar Gate in 1898 uncovered inscriptions attesting to the use of this unusual title in Macedonia, and other discoveries since have thoroughly confirmed it (see Carl Schuler, "The Macedonian Politarchs," *Classical Philology* 55, no. 2 (1960): 90–100, http://www.jstor.org). Luke was vindicated; his critics were not.

6 See F. F. Bruce, *New Testament History* (Garden City, NY: Doubleday & Co., 1969), 309.

7 These are less than half the New Testament passages containing these mingled virtues. If you would like to explore this further, here are the rest of the references: Romans 5:2; 1 Corinthians 13:2; 2 Corinthians 8:7; Ephesians 1:15–16; 6:23; Colossians 1:22–23; 1 Thessalonians 3:6; 2 Thessalonians 1:3; 1 Timothy 1:5, 13 –15; 2:15; 6:11; 2 Timothy 2:22; 3:10–11; Titus 2:1–2; Revelation 2:19.

8 For a detailed discussion of the length of Jesus' ministry, see Harold W. Hoehner, *Chronological Aspects of the Life of Christ* (Grand Rapids, MI: Zondervan, 1977), ch. 3. Hoehner provides good reasons to believe that Jesus' ministry lasted three and a half years or a bit more. Hoehner gives a much shorter discussion in his essay "Chronology," in *Dictionary of Jesus and the Gospels*, 119.

9 Judy Valente, "Father Andrew Greeley Extended Interview," *Religion and Ethics Newsweekly*, May 10, 2002, https://www.pbs.org.

10 See Mark Galli, "Speak the Gospel," *Christianity Today*, May 21, 2009, https://www.christianitytoday.com.

11 H. Müller, "Type, Pattern," in *The New International Dictionary of New Testament Theology*, edited by Colin Brown (Grand Rapids, MI: Zondervan, 1978), vol. 3, 903–907.

12 For a brief and balanced case in favor of tentmaking missions, see Ruth Siemens, "Secular Options for Missionary Work," in *Perspectives on the World Christian Movement: A Reader*, edited by Ralph Winter (Pasadena, CA: William Carey Library, 1981), 770–74.

13 In *koine* Greek, which is the original language of the New Testament books, masculine terms were often used to refer to groups consisting of both males and females. This was not a slight meant to overlook or ignore women; it was simply a linguistic convention for simplicity's sake. The same was true in English until the last half-century. For example, Jefferson's "all men are created equal" in the US Declaration of Independence connoted both men and women. Because modern readers are more sensitive to the scent of sexism, most modern translations rightly render the Greek word for *brothers* as *brothers and sisters*.

14 Even more surprisingly, the oldest textual variants we have refer to Paul as the baby sibling in the family. This may be a scribal error, but the analogy would be rich. The baby brother or sister is not characterized by authority or pride but simplicity and helplessness. Without powerful positions or family connections or local friends, the apostle and his companions came to Thessalonica as strangers without even a home of their own. Like gentle babies, they needed the fellowship of their new converts.

15 Answer key: G, F, B, H, M, N, J, K, A, L, E, C, I, D.

16 Demosthenes, "Against Neaera," in *Demosthenes*, translated by Norman W. DeWitt and Norman J. DeWitt (Cambridge, MA: Harvard University Press; London: William Heinemann Ltd., 1949), 59, 122.

17 The phrase "each of you must guard your sexual purity" (4:4) literally means "each should possess his own vessel." Some translations, like TPT, interpret this to emphasize control of one's own body, but historically, it

has been understood by some to mean "each man should take his own wife." In other words, a Christian marriage is the proper container for sexual desire. Both principles of self-control and godly Christian marriage are taught in the New Testament sexual ethic.

18 For advice on doing so, see https://www.covenanteyes.com/blog/accountability-group.

19 Erwin Lutzer, *Your Eternal Reward: Triumph and Tears at the Judgment Seat of Christ* (Chicago, IL: Moody Press, 2015); Lee Strobel, *The Case for Heaven: A Journalist Investigates Evidence for Life after Death* (Grand Rapids, MI: Zondervan, 2021); Randy Alcorn, *Heaven: A Comprehensive Guide to Everything the Bible Says about Our Eternal Home* (Wheaton, IL: Tyndale House, 2004).

20 Tim Mackie, "Book of 1 Thessalonians Summary: A Complete Animated Overview," Bible Project, November 17, 2016, https://bibleproject.com.

21 Bruce, *1 & 2 Thessalonians*, Word Biblical Commentary series (Waco, TX: Word Publishing, 1982), 120.

22 Brother Lawrence of the Resurrection, *The Practice of the Presence of God* (New York: Doubleday, 1977), 37–38.

23 For example, this is the view expressed by John Stott in his commentary *The Gospel and the End of Time: The Message of 1 & 2 Thessalonians* (Downers Grove, IL: InterVarsity Press, 1991), and by Ralph Martin in his book *Worship in the Early Church* (Grand Rapids, MI: Eerdmans, 1964).

24 See TPT, "Introduction" to 2 Thessalonians. Bruce, in his work *New Testament History,* even states that 1 & 2 Thessalonians "were written only a few weeks, or months at the most, after Paul's departure from their city" (308).

25 According to Open Doors, a Christian ministry formed "to strengthen and equip Christians around the world who are facing persecution and discrimination because of their faith in Jesus Christ." See "World Watch List: Trends," Open Doors, 2023, https://www.opendoors.org.

26 Drea Humphrey, "Close to 100 Canadian Churches Burned and/or Vandalized Since False Unmarked Grave Claim," *Rebel News*, January 3, 2024, https://www.rebelnews.com.

27 For an explanation and evaluation of preterism, see the essay by Fred Zaspel, "Preterism: Has All Prophecy Been Fulfilled?" The Gospel Coalition, accessed January 10, 2024, https://www.thegospelcoalition.org.

28 If you would like to learn more about the Christian doctrine of eschatology, here are a few resources that can get you started: Robert P. Lightner, *Last Days Handbook*, rev. ed. (Eugene, OR: Wipf & Stock, 1997, 2005); R.

Ludwigson, *A Survey of Bible Prophecy* (Grand Rapids, MI: Zondervan, 1973); Leon J. Wood, *The Bible & Future Events: An Introductory Survey of Last-Day Events* (Grand Rapids, MI: Zondervan, 1973); Ron Rhodes, *The End Times in Chronological Order* (Eugene, OR: Harvest House, 2012); Norman Geisler, *Systematic Theology: Ecclesiology, Eschatology*, vol. 4 (Grand Rapids, MI: Bethany House, 2005), Part 2; Darrell L. Bock, gen. ed., *Three Views on the Millennium and Beyond*, Counterpoints series (Grand Rapids, MI: Zondervan, 1999).

29 This is not to say that all traditions are bad; many are not, whether they are religious, political, national, ethical, or cultural. But when traditions are used to counter or obfuscate clearly evidenced truths, especially those revealed by God himself, then the traditions should yield to those truths. For more on this issue, see Jaroslav Pelikan, *The Vindication of Tradition* (New Haven, CT: Yale University Press, 1984). The issue of tradition ultimately comes down to who says, which is the subject of authority. An excellent treatment of authority is provided by Bernard Ramm in his book *The Pattern of Religious Authority* (Grand Rapids, MI: Wm. B. Eerdmans, 1959).

30 Stott, *The Gospel and the End of Time*, 178.

31 Operation World (https://operationworld.org/) is a well-researched prayer resource for learning about modern nations, their people groups, and the challenges of proclaiming the good news among them. The Joshua Project (https://joshuaproject.net/) is a similar resource specifically focusing on the groups with the fewest followers of Christ.

32 Second Thessalonians 3:6, study note 'j,' TPT.

33 For more on a Christian theology of work, see Timothy Keller with Katherine Leary Alsdorf, *Every Good Endeavor: Connecting Your Work to God's Work* (New York: Penguin Random House, 2012); Doug Sherman and William Hendricks, *Your Work Matters to God* (Colorado Springs, CO: NavPress, 1987).

34 Answer key: (1) I; (2) H; (3) L; (4) K; (5) A; (6) D; (7) F; (8) C; (9) B; (10) E; (11) G; (12) J.